Praise for *Brain Change*

"UPLIFTING. Full of passion and wisdom. Take it to heart."

- Michael Merzenich, Author of *Soft-Wired*

"BRAVO, Lyle, for extending your experienced hand to any who seek change."

- Joel T.M. Bamford
Author with Cochrane Research

"I have known Lyle for several years. I am impressed by his persistence and dedication – first, to understand and change his own brain, but then to extend this hard-won knowledge to others. I believe his book has the potential to start many people on journeys of awakening and self-discovery that will show them a way out of the various prisons life has built for them."

- Peter S Miller, MD, FRCPC
Board Certified Neuropsychiatrist

"LYLE has a remarkable ability to help others see a new path, an ability born out of the tumultuous life he had led."

- Frank Jewell, St. Louis County Commissioner

"LYLE Wildes is the most genuinely positive human being we've ever met. He believes in 'changing the world' one person at a time, and he is living proof that it can be done. Our lives have been enriched for knowing Lyle. If you do what he says, your life can change for the better as well."
- Rev. John Clark Pegg
Dr. Lyn Clark Pegg

"GETTING to know Lyle toward the end of his 20 years locked up enriched my life. These pages of getting to know him and the insights that have come through his incredible journey can enrich yours."
- Brooks Anderson, Retired Lutheran Minister
Peace and Justice Activist

"THERE is an old adage that says you can take people as far as you've gone. Lyle Wildes has traveled far. The change process he advocates is one he walked through every step of the way. Lyle has inspired many to take hold of their lives and move positively forward and he just might inspire you to do the same."
- Scott Miller, Program Coordinator
Domestic Abuse Intervention Programs

"LYLE'S understanding of the human motivation and behavior greatly benefits those that are fortunate enough to work with him. In helping to identify core values – individually and collectively – he is able to harness the positive energy present in an organization to allow for a healthy culture to prosper."

- Dave Lee, MA, LP, LMFT, LICSW, Director
Carlton County Public Health & Human Services

"THIS book holds some of the wisdom Lyle gleaned from his years of experience of creating the best quality of life for himself and those around him, no matter the circumstances."

- Carol Thompson, Ed. D.
Domestic Abuse Intervention Programs
Co-Facilitator Men's Non-Violence Program

"LYLE'S book shares his incredible life journey that inspires an exploration of how our brains can be changed and lives turned around. An important read."

- Coral McDonnell
Retired Domestic Violence Worker

BRAIN CHANGE

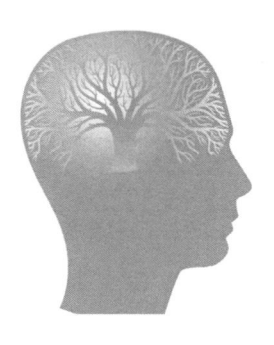

20 years growing up...
20 years messed up...
20 years locked up...
But I never gave up!

Lyle Wildes

Brain Change by Lyle Wildes

Copyright © 2016 by Lyle Wildes

All rights reserved. Printed in the United States of America.

No part of this book may be reproduced, stored in a retrieval system, or transmitted in any form, by any means, including mechanical, electronic, photocopying, recording, or otherwise, without prior written permission of the author.

To contact the author, please send correspondence to:

Lyle Wildes
P.O. Box 231
Duluth, MN 55801-0231
www.wildesbraincoach.com
Lyle@wildesbraincoach.com

ISBN: 978-0-9797614-4-7

10 9 8 7 6 5 4 3 2 1

*Dedicated to
The Mystery of Life*

Acknowledgments

Helma Wildes, my Mom, had given up on me for years but became a major influence during my early years of incarceration. She was educated and believed change was a possibility even though she ran away from a violent home, giving up on her own violent, drunken dad. Mom probably thought I was becoming her dad and gave up on me until I was stripped of my freedom. Her final words bravely claimed it was good for me to be planted in the fertile soil of loss and difficulty. Talking with her every Saturday and facing her sudden death during my incarceration was a powerful experience that clearly became a gift out of the mystery of life.

Father (Fr.) Clair Dinger, Milan Prison Chaplain, was my job supervisor seven days a week the first six years of my incarceration. At first, I had my issues with Fr. Dinger as a prison staff, but my incarceration was different because I met this unique and kind man. It was Fr. Dinger's supervisory skills that enabled me to blossom where I was planted. I was privileged to be his clerk, and the chance of that happening is also a gift from the mystery of life.

Purpose

The purpose of this book is to understand the brain's thinking as neural pathways, synapses, and chemistry acting as a systemic process. This neural network making up the brain is the sole organ of our behavior. This systemic process, or the brain, reacts to any stimuli out of the neural network at that moment. A systemic process has many areas firing together and yet does not have a central location that knows right from wrong, good or bad, or the difference between an imagined or real threat. The brain network witnesses, learns, and catches behaviors and then develops pathways, synapses, and chemistry to support those behavioral patterns. When the brain is exposed to different environments, it can respond inappropriately. When it does, we may erroneously focus on punishing rather than coaching the brain to relearn new and appropriate behaviors.

Understanding the brain as a systemic process is radically different from some religious notions of the brain housing a Self susceptible to selfishness and greed; and then, down deep, it clearly knows right from wrong. Some religious circles support the notion of freewill and an awakened Self fully capable and responsible for overcoming its corrupted nature to "do the right thing." It is my claim that many brains are exposed to emotional and physical abuse, gang violence, violent sports, wars, tumors, and accidents that may damage the brain's neurological network.

Changing the brain can cause different behaviors related to the brain damage, changed chemistry, and neural activity. If we view the brain as a systemic process not knowing good from bad and also the sole

BRAIN CHANGE

organ of our behavior, it will require a change in the way we treat our offspring, each other, and antisocial behavior. Accepting brain change and the importance of coaching the brain, rather than punishing it, will be the focus of this book and the challenge for many in the 21st century.

20 years growing up...

"My brain developed a neurological landscape that supported my learned values and beliefs."

- Lyle Wildes

My brain, the one writing this book, acquired its infrastructure during its nine-month prenatal period. Then, after passing through my mother's birth canal, my brain marinated in the stories and experiences of my family's lifestyle and the culture of my rural community. My developing brain was exposed to the telling of legends, folklore, mythologies, cosmologies, and theologies. It caught the values and beliefs of my parents, community members, and the teachings of a protestant church. These experiences activated and strengthened certain neurological pathways in my brain. Other possible pathways were not activated, causing them to shrink and become purged.

BRAIN CHANGE

My brain developed its unique neurological network as a result from being raised on a small farm in Wisconsin. Our farm was nestled in a valley where a small stream originated and flowed down through the pasture for our twenty milking cows. Fields spread up both sides above the pasture with many hickory trees topping off the hillsides. I enjoyed the smells of the many bushes and wild flowers. I witnessed many breathtaking sunrises, sunsets, and star-filled evening skies. I was isolated on this small farm where we raised most everything we ate. I learned about planting, cultivating, and harvesting crops in the fields as well as the various vegetables and fruits from our garden and fruit trees. Many lessons were caught during my everydayness on the farm with my family. Sex was considered a risky act for pregnancy and not to be done for enjoyment. My brain learned many different behaviors related to the treatment of animals and what we defined as weeds on our small farm. If we were invited to a public bonfire and cookout, I was often corrected on my social behavior. My brain became the organ of my habitual small farm culture. This learned or socialization process determined my character before I had a chance to evaluate the kind of person I wanted to BE. I mimicked what I witnessed over the first twenty years of my life. It became habitual or automatic and I never felt a need to change. I grew more accustomed to being Lyle. However, I was often punished for inappropriate behavior during my early years in grade school.

Later in my life, I tried to become a bank employee and I often felt awkward, and at times angry, in the various changing social situations. The values and beliefs I caught from my parents focused on vocational skills necessary for survival and little attention to public life, philosophy, or self reflection. My parents exposed me to a world where I was constantly in battle with Satan who was always enticing and tempting me to do evil. I was taken to the Methodist church where I interacted with other farm kids who thought a lot like me. By now my brain was running on automatic pilot and I didn't need to reflect on my behavior. I associated and identified with other kids like myself and in some cases disliked or judged those different from me. My mental process locked me into a way of life where my ability to think, understand

BRAIN CHANGE

and blossom was limited. The sky was not the limit for this young boy named Lyle Wildes. My focus in life was more about pleasing God and becoming good at physical skills and not about the values and beliefs that were passed on to me as times changed, limiting what I could become. For the first twenty years of my life growing up I lived out the character given to me with limiting results. My learned values and beliefs were causing chaos and I couldn't begin to understand why I continuously felt unfinished.

After high school I worked for a couple of years as a banker and suddenly sabotaged my banking future. I again felt In-Between. I applied to the University of Wisconsin-Platteville where I was accepted and given a full wrestling scholarship. Soon after arriving on campus, the wrestling coach asked me to wrestle the A-Team wrestler in my weight division. I wrestled him at our high school conference championship where I pinned him in the first round. The match ended in a tie. The coach told me I had to beat him to get on the team. I told the coach I hadn't wrestled for over two years and my passion for wrestling was gone. I was not going to invest my life in becoming a great wrestler. He started yelling and screaming so I simply walked out of the gym, sad and confused. While walking back to my car I was going through the student center just as a small, thin man was leaving. As if out of the mystery of life the man asked,

"Are you okay?"

I openly confessed I was going to drop out of college because I couldn't find what was missing in my life. He smiled and asked if I would be willing to attend one of his classes before I left.

"Why not? Sure," I said.

When I arrived at the classroom I was certain I was in the wrong room and turned to leave. Dr. Hood, the professor who invited me, was coming up the hallway. I stepped toward him and whispered,

"You want me to go in there, with all those crazy looking people?"

He smiled again and said,

"Everything will be okay. Just come on inside."

I went in and sat in the back of the room. Everyone else was sitting up front as if expecting something exciting was about to happen. As I found my seat Professor Hood told the class I was having a difficult time finding what was missing in my life. Everyone looked back at me and laughed and said something like "join the club" in unison.

Professor Hood started giving a lecture on Plato's allegory of the cave and asked how we know what is simply an opinion, true opinion, knowledge, or wisdom. What we have learned could just be our parents' opinion, it could be a true opinion, a belief, a value, or maybe even wisdom, but it could not be a truth that gives us permission to kill in support. At that point I instantly felt like I was home. I jumped up and yelled,

"Yes, this is what I need to talk about. What are values, beliefs, attitudes, and truths? And is there a God?"

Everyone turned and looked at me. One of the female students looked back at the professor and made a mark in the air as if to say,

"Another one hooked, Professor."

Everyone laughed and Dr. Hood continued to lecture. When the class was over, Dr. Hood wanted to talk with me about my interest in philosophy. I didn't even know what the word philosophy meant, but I knew I had found my home. When I told

BRAIN CHANGE

Mom about my experience, she trusted I was where I needed to be at this time in my life. After all, she just wanted me to find what I was missing so I wouldn't live life feeling unfinished. Mom couldn't tell me what I needed, but she certainly pointed me in the right direction. After Dr. Hood talked with me he realized I had come out of a religious mess. He was concerned that studying philosophy could cause me to fall into nihilistic delusion or become lost in meaninglessness. He had been a professor of philosophy long enough to know the challenges students like me face when searching for what is missing in their lives.

While adjusting to all of these changes, Glenda, my girlfriend of two years, transferred to the Platteville campus to finish her degree in education. We were married the summer before we graduated from college. She was planning to be a grade school teacher and I had hopes of being a high school sociology teacher in the same district while working toward my Master's degree. We lived in a remote area on the edge of the city of Platteville in a small cabin when our lives suddenly changed on Friday, January 16, 1971. This ended my twenty years of growing up and began my twenty years of being messed up.

* * *

During these first twenty years, my brain developed a neurological network to habitually mimic the behaviors of my brain coaches. I believe repeated experiences gave my brain its values and beliefs which seem suspended in the midst of my brain's neurological network.

As a newborn child my brain yearned to understand its surroundings. During this process, my brain accepted the stories and explanations of the world in which it was told. My developing brain didn't know the difference between what is real and what was myth. The coaching and storytelling all happened when my brain was very young, innocent, accepting, and extremely curious. The stories I heard were contagious and easily caught by my attentive brain without an internal mechanism to critically evaluate them. The atmosphere in my home was filled with many of the puritan Christian stories. My brain was told and accepted the Christian God story, the seven day Creation story, and the Santa Claus story. To coach a young brain to believe what is simply not true one also had to believe the brain had an inner ability to eventually demystify myths through a prior knowing of the truth. In other words, the brain was thought to have an inner homunculus that knows right from wrong. However, my brain created a neurological profile to support what my caregivers taught me; my brain then resisted and filtered out all conflicting evidence. God and Santa really existed in my world and I witnessed their presence and works in public displays. There was no doubt in my brain that God and Santa were real.

On the other hand, my brother's brain initially accepted the God and Santa story but also began to accept conflicting evidence. His brain slowly started doubting the God and Santa stories. He openly noticed flaws in the story and mentally transformed those lessons about God and Santa from reality to myths with no harm done to his world view or cosmology. However, my brain filtered out all conflicting evidence and held the God and Santa story as truth until social pressure drove me to consult the one I trusted most – my mom. Those of us with

BRAIN CHANGE

the neurological network to fully support and trust our caregivers' stories did not have the neurological ability to demystify or deconstruct those same myths. When I was driven to confront Mom, she made light of my question, expecting I would demystify the Santa story on my own. But when I persisted, she painfully and surprisingly realized I had not demystified the Santa story. Instead, I had totally accepted it, believed it, and even defended it. She got down on one knee and gently looked into my frightened eyes as her terrifying words rippled through my brain. Her lips mouthed the news and my brain struggled to filter out their meaning. I backed away feeling betrayed, angry, alone, and disappointed. I felt my brain had became hijacked. I felt vulnerable, scared, confused, and insecure. I believed her story and I didn't have the brain equipment to demystify it on my own.

Could there be a continuum of neurological landscapes that allow the brain to get caught more strongly than others? To address this question, we must understand the brain's infrastructure lacking freewill and knowing right from wrong. Today we still refuse to believe there are various brain

BRAIN CHANGE

neurological landscapes that can build trust and other brain landscapes designed to be skeptical, open to doubting myths, legends, and religious stories.

20 years messed up...

"Since your accident you're not the son I raised."

- Helma Wildes

I worked my way through college repairing and delivering appliances for Bob Weygant's appliance store in Platteville, WI. January 16, 1971, I delivered a stove and dishwasher near the little town of New Diggings, WI. I was traveling back to the store on unfamiliar roads much too fast when I realized I was approaching a hairpin corner. I applied the brakes and began skidding down an icy road as the bridge was slowly lining up. My vehicle was floating toward a concrete bridge abutment. The abutment kept coming and coming and eventually hit the front of the car. The grill was crushed and the engine plowed inside the car. The right side of the steering wheel collapsed and my seat belt unfastened, causing my head and shoulders to slam forward, hitting the steering wheel. My brain experienced a serious concussion from hitting the bridge, driving my four front teeth into the steering wheel. My skull was instantly cracked like a dropped egg causing my brain to be slammed around, putting me out like a light.

I awoke in a panic. I broke my teeth off and opened the driver's side door. I can still hear the creaking sounds of the car door opening. I climbed out and started running to a nearby house to call my boss. Fading in and out, I remember running to the house and then running toward the car, seeing the house and seeing the car but never getting close to the house or away from the car. A local farmer came upon the scene and took me to the hospital in Hazel Green, WI. My wife, Glenda, and Robert and Alice Weygant were waiting at the hospital when we arrived. I ran to the hospital and collapsed into a waiting wheel chair. The last words I remember were Mr. Weygant saying to his wife,

"Come on, let's go home. He'll never survive."

When regaining my presence in time and space, the first thing I heard was the local doctor talking to my wife of four months.

"I am sorry, Mrs. Wildes, but your husband is gone."

"Oh my God, I'm dead."

As I lay there, helpless, I thought,

"Either death is different than I expected or I have a poor doctor."

I squeezed my frightened wife's hand to let her know I was still alive.

"Doctor, Lyle just squeezed my hand."

The doctor had already concluded that I was dead so his response was,

"Oh, that's probably death spasms."

Oh God, now I'm going to die of negligence. To my joy, the doctor then slowly moved his hand down my neck to check for a pulse. At last, he stated,

"His pulse is back. We have to rush him to the Mercy Hospital in Dubuque, IA."

The last thing I heard was the doctor telling my wife,

"Lyle is probably better off dead. With damage like that to his head, he will never be the same."

The folks at the Mercy Hospital saved my life, and I cannot thank them enough for their kindness and quality of work. Again and again, my presence was compromised and I can't remember anything during the next few days. Suddenly, out of nowhere I heard the phone ring in my room. An elderly nurse answered the phone and referred to the caller as Mrs. Wildes.

"No, your son is in a coma. He cannot speak."

I tugged at the nurse's uniform. She looked at me, shocked and confused, and I motioned for her to hand me the phone.

"Hi, Mom."

Hearing my voice, Mom believed I was okay. However, that night the radio reported that Lyle Wildes was in critical condition in the Mercy Hospital in Dubuque, IA. Mom and Dad packed their car and drove south over two hours to the Mercy Hospital. When they arrived, Mom walked to my bed and said,

"You little brat, you could have died and we would have heard about it over the radio. Why didn't someone tell us you were hurt this bad?"

I lay there thinking,

"What does she mean, this bad?"

I could move all the parts of my body, but I had a headache that would not go away. Mom talked to my doctor and he assured her I would be okay in a few days. I don't know how much time passed, but later my doctors came into the room and asked me a few routine questions.

"What is your name? Who are your parents? When is your birthday?"

Having answered these questions correctly, the doctors decided that my brain was not damaged and that it could process my future with the same level of compassion and empathy prior to the accident. They were wrong! My relationship with my surroundings changed instantly. I was now impatient, disorganized, and careless. Daily life didn't feel any different to me, but I lost connection to my old friends, goals, and interests.

With only a few weeks until graduation, I realized I didn't like my new wife, Glenda, nor did I want to sit by her during my graduation. Glenda was confused and devastated over my new attitude. She called her mother who drove from Sauk City, WI, down to Platteville to be with her. They then called my mom and asked what was happening with me. My mom knew nothing about my new attitude and asked,

"What's this not liking anyone all

about?"

"I don't have feelings for Glenda anymore and I'm not attending my graduation ceremony either. I don't want to sit beside her during the ceremony."

"Since your accident you're not the son I raised. What's wrong with you?"

My parents saw me as flawed and never considered neurological brain damage as the cause of my new behavior. They threatened to disown me if I didn't "shape up." In the fog of my rattled brain, I decided to find a doctor who would give me a vasectomy so my parents would never become grandparents by me. Even though I was acting careless, everything felt proper and right. My brain had slammed inside my skull, altering its shape and mode of operation. In an instant my brain was changed, as was the quality of my life. My brain's landscape was altered, causing a lack of interest in the same goals or dreams I had prior to my accident.

When Glenda received the divorce papers she was shocked and confused. She called her mom, her mom called my mom, and Mom called me to ask what was wrong. I told her things had changed and I didn't understand why. I assured Mom I didn't like

BRAIN CHANGE

her, either. I still remember the sound of Mom crying on the phone; she didn't know what to do with her son's new attitude.

As the swelling of my skull gradually receded, my broken and chipped teeth needed to be extracted or crowned. My skull had cracked like a dropped egg and shifted an eighth of an inch, causing a need for facial and nose reconstruction. I was scheduled to be put under local anesthesia for surgery. When I arrived I was told to sit in the dentist chair as Dr. White and his assistant started clamping my arms and legs down. When I asked why, I was told they didn't want me to reach for my face or move my legs during surgery. That made sense, but they continued clamping down my thighs and my chest and finally strapped my head against the head rest. The only movement possible was moving my toes, fingers, my eyes and my mouth. In a frank tone of voice Dr. White said,

"We will not be putting you under local anesthesia. Instead, we are going to freeze your face and keep you awake so you don't suffocate from blood coagulating in your throat."

Without my approval, Dr. White

picked up a device with an attached needle that looked six inches long. In spite of my objections, he penetrated the needle into my face causing pain I didn't think I could endure. It only took a few minutes, but it felt like hours. Then Dr. White and the nurse stood by my side, waiting for the numbness to overtake my face. As this happened I noticed a strong taste in the back of my mouth which I remembered from prior dentist office visits. When I asked Dr. White about the unusually strong taste he said it was the agent they were using to freeze my face. Prior to this experience I had not altered my brain with any drugs, chemicals, or alcohol. As I sat in the chair a euphoric feeling emerged in my head. My body tingled and I felt uninhibited and talkative.

I looked up at Dr. White and asked if he was married. He was. I asked the nurse if she was married. She was, too. I then asked if they were married to each other and the answer was no. I suspiciously moved my eyes back and forth between them both, then asked if they were having an affair. The nurse gave a gentle slap on my shoulder and said,

"Mr. Wildes!"

BRAIN CHANGE

I explained how beautiful she was and that I was attracted to her. Dr. White put his fingers on my moving lips and said,

"Mr. Wildes, I see what this agent does to you and if you keep talking we'll have to tape your mouth shut."

I looked back to the nurse. She was smiling and said,

"Thank you for the compliment, Mr. Wildes."

During the painful surgery, I faded off into this artificial inner euphoric experience that I would remember and eventually seek out again.

* * *

Following a number of surgeries and still graduating with degrees in Philosophy and Sociology from University of Wisconsin-Plattcville campus, I was admitted to graduate school at the Pacific School of Religion (PSR). PSR was part of the Graduate Theological Union in Berkeley, CA. I attended classes for a short time but couldn't focus and didn't give the professors any respect. It became obvious I had to drop out and I then returned to Wisconsin. When

BRAIN CHANGE

I arrived back at Wisconsin, I was asked to substitute at the University of Wisconsin-Richland Center campus for a Philosophy professor who had a serious heart attack earlier in the semester. I wasn't there long until I decided I didn't like the students either. After getting frustrated I walked into the classroom one day and broke up most of the chalk and wrote on the chalk board,

"Class has been cancelled do to a lack of interest."

I grabbed a sturdy yardstick and slapped my desk and ordered everyone out of my classroom. The twenty students started yelling and running out the door. I followed them, slapping the wall with my stick yelling,

"Get out and don't come back."

I returned to my classroom and gently picked up my belongings and went home. I wasn't there long until the president of the college was at my door. She asked if everything was okay and I assured her everything was fine. After some rather heated conversation I was ordered back to class to finish out the semester. I went back and told the students all they had to do was write a paper about the philosopher they liked best and why. I didn't feel I had done anything wrong or unusual.

As the saying goes, when one door closes another one opens. At this time my brother and his wife came to Richland Center to encourage me to get into the mobile home transportation business with them. My brother talked with me while my date and I were bowling at the Richland Center bowling alley. He told me he had already expanded the business into two sales lots and there were over thirty more we could service. He asked,

"How about you and I become partners and take over the mobile home delivery operation in Wisconsin?"

"Unfortunately, I can't now."

"Why not?"

"I have to finish teaching this semester."

"Lyle, this business is going to go big and quickly. We can make a fortune by doing this together. How much do you make working for the University?"

"Well, I just got my first check and it looks like I will be taking home about $400 a week."

"We could make more than a grand a day. How much longer do you have to teach?"

I left the academic community and became partners with my brother. We became the first mobile home transportation company to move a mobile home from one location to another and have it ready to live in the same day. Prior to us, protocol was seven to nine days. The customers expected to move in immediately and no service provider thought it possible or necessary to set up a mobile home in one day. We discovered there were no licenses needed to make all the necessary connections. Thus, we created a same day turnkey delivery service. Our business developed faster than we could find and train trusted drivers. During expansion of our business, my brother thought I was too antisocial because I wouldn't drink a beer with my customers after setting up their new home. He felt we bonded better with our clients if we had a beer with them to celebrate our work and their satisfaction. He expected me to drink socially even though I didn't drink, do drugs, or party with him or anyone else.

One winter Friday evening I dressed up

and went out alone to get drunk. I had no idea what this experience was going to feel like since I had never drank or did drugs before. I drove to the Richland Center bowling alley since the city of Richland Center was a dry town. After sitting down at the bar I had no idea what to order. I sat beside a businessman and decided to mimic him. When the bartender asked what I wanted to drink I pointed to the businessman's drink and said,

"I'll have one of those."

I later learned it was a brandy old fashioned sweet. It was filled with booze, ice, fruit, and an interesting stir stick making it look like a healthy drink. I watched the businessman pensively stir his drink so I copied him by nibbling on the fruit. When I eventually took a sip I thought,

"Hmm, not bad."

I continued sipping my drink as did the businessman. When he ordered another I did, too. After completing my second drink I ordered a third. A few sips into my third drink I had to go to the bathroom. I stepped down off my bar stool and orientated myself. I could feel the effects and started to experience a wonderful euphoric feeling.

BRAIN CHANGE

As I stood in front of the urinal I was in a mental state of joy. I felt alive like I had felt only once before. I returned to my bar stool and took another sip before initiating a conversation with the businessman and then with others at the bar. I felt free and open to everyone. After finishing my third drink, the businessman said it was time for him to leave the bar so I left the bar, too. As I drove back to my apartment I couldn't understand why my parents didn't want me to get drunk and enjoy this wonderful feeling or experience. I had lost my feeling of being unfinished and I liked it. A few days before Christmas, my brother pulled up beside me in the shopping mall parking lot in Baraboo, WI. He pulled a brown bag out from the back seat of his Lincoln Mark IV and said,

"Lyle, it's the Christmas season. Let's enjoy a little Christian Brothers."

I took a couple of swallows and my brother innocently asked,

"You started drinking?"

I was proud to admit I had.

"Well now that you're drinking I want you to remember this forever."

"What's that?"

"When you drink you will think you're

BRAIN CHANGE

much smarter then you actually are and you will also think you're tougher, too. If you remember these two things you will be okay drinking."

I flashed back on my feelings in the bowling alley and the time I had surgery following my accident. I felt uninhibited, smarter, and tougher both times. However, this was the first time I was given advice to monitor my inner feelings and thoughts. I never forgot my brother's advice and wondered why my parents never wanted us to drink and experience this unique feeling, if we just monitored our brain's thinking.

As the years passed I became bored with the success of our mobile home trucking business and decided to search for the agent of my wonderful euphoric feeling during my surgery. I sought out street cocaine but never felt that wonderful feeling so I decided to research for the agent or chemical Dr. White used during my surgery.

I finally found the real deal. Richard Willstätter discovered the structure of the synthetic cocaine molecule in 1905. The formula for manufacturing synthetic cocaine was available in three libraries in the United States and one happened to be in Wisconsin. I found it on what was then called microfiche. I wasn't sure how to get a copy printed off without drawing attention to myself, but when I asked the clerk how to get a copy of something she said,

"Just insert dimes for each page and it will print out right over there."

Wow, I could print out the 60 pages and no one would even know. I had it. There was only one problem. It was in German. I had to get it translated. I had a professor friend who was fluent in German and English and the rest of the story is history. Working with my chemist friend in Kansas City I was set to overcome my boredom and regain the thrill I had once experienced.

* * *

After my accident I had a series of short-term relationships because I could never feel connected to anyone. In 1977, my life took another turn. It started on a wet rainy summer day when I was scheduled to repossess a mobile home out of the mobile home park called Twin Oaks near Whitewater, WI. While getting the home ready to transport in the rain, I noticed an attractive woman next door. We didn't talk during that time, but a few days later I was rescheduled in the same park to repossess another mobile home on the other side of her home. This time I noticed her walking down the street in tight shorts and a beautiful top. I spoke to her when she passed and we exchanged a few words. Because of the amount of work I was scheduled each day, I didn't have much free time for chitchat nor did I want to talk. Surprisingly, I was scheduled to deliver a new mobile home and set it up next to her lot. This would take most the day.

Out of our fourteen drivers I wondered why I was randomly being exposed to this attractive woman so many times in only a few weeks. There were two hundred and fifty mobile home sites with many open spots in this park, but I went to the same two sites in a matter of days. I began to think it was another gift out of the mystery of life and I should get to know this woman. I found out during my conversation with her neighbor she was recently divorced. I initiated a conversation with her as I was packing up my tools getting ready to leave. For several days afterward, I often thought about this mysterious woman in Whitewater, WI.

BRAIN CHANGE

One Saturday, I decided to go back down to Whitewater and meet the woman who had caught my interest. I didn't know anything about her or what she might like. To cover all the bases, I decided to take a Bible, two bottles of wine, and a joint. I rehearsed my opening lines during the two hour drive.

"Hi, my name is Lyle Wildes and I have a bottle of wine, a Bible, and a joint in the car. Which would you like to use to get to know each other?"

I never thought this was strange. I arrived and knocked on her door. A young woman appeared with bobby pins in her hair. She looked young enough to be the daughter, so I asked if her mom was home. She looked amused and cocked her head to one side as she asked,

"Who are you looking for?"

"I'm looking for the woman that lives here."

"What do you want?"

Despite my rehearsal, I was thrown off course. I started to race through my introduction when she interrupted me.

"I know who you are. You're the trailer guy."

"I brought a Bible, a bottle of wine, and

a joint with me and was wondering which you would like me to bring in to get to know you better."

She looked stunned as I waited for her answer. It felt like an hour passed before she finally said,

"Bring in the wine. I have my own pot."

I dashed back to my car and returned to a closed door. When I knocked I heard,

"C'mon in."

When I entered I was stunned to see a handsome young man sitting on her kitchen counter.

"What's your name again?"

"Lyle."

"Lyle, this is my husband."

"H-h-hello," I stammered.

This wasn't what I expected. I quickly gathered myself and said,

"Look, I feel like a fool. Your neighbor said you were divorced."

"Well, we did break up but now we're back together again."

"Okay, that's great. I'll just excuse myself. Sorry for the misunderstanding."

"Wait, don't you want to share your wine?" she insisted.

Her husband smiled and said,

BRAIN CHANGE

"I think we could all use a drink."

"Okay. What the heck?"

I didn't bring a cork remover and she didn't have one. The three of us laughed as we chipped and finally pushed the cork inside. She poured three glasses of wine and started telling her husband about the day I pulled the first mobile home out in the rain. During our first glass of wine she asked,

"Why would you drive all the way down here to meet me? You're from the New Lisbon area, aren't you?"

"Yes, the Dells area. I thought you would be an interesting woman to get to know."

It wasn't long and she noted,

"We drank all your wine, Lyle."

She chuckled when I said,

"I have another bottle in the car."

To my surprise she said,

"If you want to get it, I'll roll us a joint."

Shortly after refilling our glasses, her phone rang. She gracefully walked across the room and answered it.

"It's for you."

She handed the phone to her husband. He didn't talk long before hanging the phone up. He said,

"I have to leave soon."

Time passed quickly and the phone rang again.

"It's probably for you so answer it," she demanded.

This time he seemed upset and said,

"I have to leave now."

"I have to leave, too," I stated.

She turned to her husband and asked,

"Should we tell him the truth?"

"What do you mean tell me the truth?"

Her husband agreed and said,

"I think we have put him through enough."

"OK," she says. "This isn't my husband; he's my brother-in-law. He came over today to check out the tires for my mobile home. I am selling my house, too. When you went to get the wine I asked him to stay. I didn't know who you were or what you were up to. You can stay and finish the wine with me if you would like."

After he left, I asked,

"Would you like to go out for dinner?"

Unfortunately, she had a date coming from St. Paul, MN.

"Maybe we could do it another time?"

She gave me her phone number and I returned home. I waited a few days before

BRAIN CHANGE

I called and asked if she would go out with me.

"I would like that."

That's how our relationship started. One day she asked me to hold her nine-month-old child, Jed. As I was holding him, he seemed to be smiling at me. Jed and I had a connection and over a period of a few months she agreed to cut all her ties and move her family to Wisconsin Dells to be with me. I didn't like or dislike the idea, but I agreed to the suggestion. She sold her mobile home and moved to Wisconsin Dells with her three children. She left everything behind and trusted our relationship would be safe and long-lasting. She got her bus driver's license and started driving a school bus for the Wisconsin Dells School District. She loved her job and I think she actually loved me, too. She never had a chance to develop some good women friends in the Dells area.

It was during this time I became an active underground chemist in Juneau County. I took advantage of her situation and became physically and mentally abusive. This chaos continued until one day she had enough. She was done with my violence and apathy. She called the cops and as they were coming up the driveway she informed me I could either move out tonight or she was going to expose my illegal operation. Knowing that she feared me I felt assured I wasn't moving out and she wasn't going to do any such thing. I was wrong. I was moved out, arrested, and charged with manufacturing a controlled substance.

When they busted me they had no idea of the sophistication of my lab operation. However, I was in the process of moving my operation to Kansas City and had boxed most of the lab equipment and chemicals. The State of Wisconsin found a lot of the equipment and most of the chemicals. Because they didn't find any precursors, I claimed I had ended my project. I didn't think they could charge me with attempting only to manufacture a controlled substance, but they did. The state was not in a hurry to prosecute me and waited for me to get caught up in another drug deal.

It wasn't long and I was arrested again, this time for aiding and abetting in the delivery of pot. With two charges pending the state decided to take me to trial on the manufacturing case. We went to trial and I

BRAIN CHANGE

claimed I had ceased my illegal operation and was no longer working as an underground chemist. The jury didn't believe me and found me guilty.

Richard Surgess, my attorney, complained about having a headache throughout the trial. He wasn't the aggressive and professional lawyer I knew and hired earlier. After my trial, my attorney returned to Milwaukee and died from metastasized cancer in his brain. This left me without an attorney, and my aiding and abetting case was still pending. A few weeks later, the individual I was supposed to have aided and abetted was acquitted. What a relief! How could I be charged with aiding and abetting a crime if the defendant was found not guilty of the crime?

My new attorney took my case and wanted me to agree to plea to the aiding and abetting case. He told me I could be found guilty of a crime where the defendant I aided and abetted was acquitted. He told me my jury could find me guilty because they believed the jury that acquitted my co-defendant was wrong. He convinced me, and I signed a plea agreement that would consolidate both cases into one case with one sentence. This plea agreement would give me one felony and a four-year sentence. On the other hand, if the judge sentenced me to both cases and ran my sentences consecutively, it could be ten years.

* * *

My new attorney didn't file the paperwork required for the plea agreement. As a result, I was sentenced in two different courts to two different sentences. I was given three and a half years for attempting to manufacture a controlled substance and another four years for aiding and abetting in the delivery of a controlled substance. Both sentences were to run concurrent. I was taken to Wisconsin DOC admissions located in Dodge, WI. From there I was designated to the maximum security prison in Waupun, WI despite receiving a sentence of only four years for what was considered a nonviolent, victimless crime.

A few weeks after I was incarcerated, I asked Jed's mom if she would bring Jed to visit me. I was the only Dad Jed knew and I believed he should visit me so he didn't imagine me involved in all the craziness he saw on TV. Even though he was only eight, I knew he needed to see me safe so he could put his fears to rest. After an extended debate, she agreed but only if I promised not to create a scene. I agreed and the following visiting day she brought Jed to visit me. The look on Jed's face remains so clear in my memory, it causes tears as I write these painful words.

"I'm really glad you came today, Jed."

"Me too, Dad."

I pulled my khaki collar open and said,

"See Jed, daddy's not hurt. I'm safe and we will be together again."

"Okay," Jed said, wiping the tears from his eyes.

"Jed, do you want to know a few things about prison?"

Jed's face lit up.

"Daddy works as a clerk in arts and crafts and I get to meet some unique people here in prison."

"Like who, Dad?"

"Some play harmonicas, do bead work, ceramics, play guitar, and there's this really unique guy named Billy."

"Does he play the guitar, Daddy?"

"No, he's an artist. He's drawing a

BRAIN CHANGE

mural on one of the walls in the arts and crafts room. It is going to be nine feet high and 30 feet long."

"Wow, what's he drawing?"

"It looks as if you and I are sitting on a boat looking at the shoreline. He's got stores in the background and tables sitting out in front of the stores as if on a sidewalk. The sidewalk comes out to the beach and the water comes splashing up against the side of the sidewalk. He has a flag blowing the same direction as the scarves and the hair of people sitting at the tables. He even has droplets of splashing water flying in front of the people."

"Wow. Can we go see it, Dad?"

"No, we can't go in, Jed. But maybe I can send you a picture of it. There are some news reporters who might be coming down for the unveiling of the mural. Everyone just loves it."

After a moment of silence the officer walked up.

"You're time is up, inmate Wildes."

"Is everything okay in school, Jed?"

"Yep."

"Dad will be out soon, Son. Stay happy."

Jed hugged me tight and said,

"I love you, Daddy."

Jed's mom gave me a hug and grabbed Jed's hand and said,

"I'll see you when you get out."

Watching them walk off, I couldn't stop the tears and feeling of guilt about how Jed felt and angry about being locked up.

* * *

I was behind the walls of Waupun for a couple of weeks when a lieutenant approached my cell. He was standing there with his white shirt and lieutenant hat looking soberly into my cell. He firmly stated,

"Inmate, I will be calling you out later in the week."

I kept thinking,

"Why would the lieutenant need to call me out?"

When I was escorted to his office I was shocked to realize I knew him. He owned one of the mobile home sales lots. When we were alone in his office he asked me,

"What are you doing in here?"

I looked back at him and asked,

"What the fuck are you doing as a

lieutenant in a prison? You bought stolen goods from us and were always on the edge of the law, and now you're a prison lieutenant? What's wrong with this picture?"

He smiled and continued,

"Lyle, there can be some serious violence behind these walls and I am asking you to let me know if you hear anything. Okay?"

Being in the mindset of a convict, I told him he had picked his side and I picked mine.

"Don't expect me to snitch on anyone who is on my side. Now, Mr. Lieutenant, I must leave your office or the other inmates will think we have something going on and that could be a problem for me."

The lieutenant never bothered me again. He knew we had a past that could cost him his job.

I was behind those walls for roughly thirteen months until I was transferred to a medium security prison in Fox Lake, WI. Three powerful memories often come to mind as a result of my stay in Waupun:

First, a young man a couple of cells down from me was attacked while locked in his cell. I had been typing briefs for a prisoner who was our third-level tier tender. The tier

BRAIN CHANGE

tender told me it would be best if I took a nap this afternoon about 2:00 pm. I didn't know why, but at 2:00 pm I got up on my wire bed and took a nap. That afternoon three balloons filled with gas were thrown into a young man's cell followed by a lit match. As the balloons busted the match ignited the gas. I awoke to the blast and a flash on the prison wall and then screams from this young man. The oxygen was burning out of his cell and he was gasping and screaming for help. He fought for his life and lost before the officers were able to reach him. The guards carried him out on the cat walk past my cell. I saw his skin smoking as the officers tried to keep his face covered. This young man violated the prison underground culture and was killed for it. That experience made my comments to the prison lieutenant real and changed my prison experience at Waupun forever.

Second, Billy painted a scene that could be appreciated from any distance or angle. The mural was alive with detail. You could hear the water splashing against the wooden shoreline. Beautiful men and women walked along the beach, shading their skin with umbrellas. Billy even had a man standing at

BRAIN CHANGE

a table waving out to us.

It was Billy's greatest moment when his mural was unveiled and the media was there to record it. Billy explained to everyone the temperature of the day and how the breeze across the surface of the water was blowing at the same speed through the ladies' hair. He explained the time of day and the mood of the community. Billy saw it all simultaneously. I gave thanks for being able to share this moment in Billy's life.

As the days faded after the unveiling of his mural, Billy was getting anxious from the loss of excitement about his work. He was getting edgy. His attention span was short and he became frustrated. One day the arts and craft female supervisor came to work and was going from table to table making suggestions to each inmate about their work. Billy was sitting off alone in a daze. It took a few minutes for everyone to notice that Billy was openly masturbating. He stood up with his erect penis in his hand and began running around the room stroking his penis and repeating crazy sounds and gibberish. We were all frozen in disbelief. The supervisor dialed the deuces, a series of "two's" pushed on her radio signaling for

BRAIN CHANGE

help. Billy ejaculated into the air and stood locked as his energy faded and he appeared confused. The guards rushed into the arts and crafts room and approached Billy. The guards dragged Billy out as if he was dead. The supervisor collected herself and left the area. Billy was the talk of the compound for months.

As I sat in my cell I wondered how the best and the worst could appear in one brain. I recalled the stories Billy told me about his childhood. Billy told how his parents would blow pot smoke into their dog's face until the dog stumbled and had to lay down. Billy also told me how his parents would blow pot smoke in his face when he was a young boy. He explained how the world would become distorted for him. Billy talked about how his parents gave him beer and LSD so they could laugh when he tried to walk. He remembered laying on the floor unable to get up while his parents were on their sofa making love. When Billy came to prison as a teenager, he was confused about which state of consciousness was reality. He talked about how he didn't know what was normal in any situation. Was his behavior normal to him but horrific for us and the prison staff?

BRAIN CHANGE

I wondered,

"Did a genius get thrown into a human junkyard?"

Third, about a year into my sentence I first noticed how the noise in each cell bounced off the surrounding concrete walls. When you flushed the toilet in your cell everyone could hear it throughout the building. Every sound was magnified. One night I was laying on my wire bunk bed trying to identify all the different sounds. I heard someone on the other side of the island of cells inside our huge concrete building yell,

"Hey, 10 Speed, want to play chess?"

He was called 10 Speed because he only stole 10 speed bikes.

"Sure, let me get the board out."

As they were setting up their boards I could hear another prisoner reading a letter. I couldn't make out what he was saying, but I knew he was reading a Dear John letter because he was blowing his nose a lot. Then the chess players came back into the cacophony. I heard 10 Speed yell,

"I am moving 12 to 16."

His listening opponent was silent and then yelled,

"You can't move like that, you idiot."

BRAIN CHANGE

I realized they had numbered the boards in their cells so they could call out their moves. They would move their opponent's pieces in their cell as their opponent yelled out their move. How ingenious. As the evening grew into night, I started to hear a different texture in the atmosphere. I heard men getting ready to lie down on their wire bunks and saying their final words before going to sleep. I heard prayer after prayer begin and end. They were asking God to protect their children, protect them, have the judge give a favorable ruling on their appeal. For the first time I imagined all the prayers being uttered in prisons, hospitals, army bases throughout the world and in different languages. As I listened to all the prayers, I realized God couldn't possibly grant all the various prayers. Some prayers were conflictual. How could the America soldier have his prayer answered when the opponent soldier was praying for their own victory and safety to the same God? How could the prisoner be released if he had actually hurt another person and it was proven beyond the reason of doubt?

As I listened to all the prayers and sounds of crying voices, the atmosphere was slowly filling with the sound of crying men and a moaning harmonica. The harmonica became louder and louder until it filled the building with the sounds of agony, pain, sadness, and hopelessness. I laid on my wire bunk and promised I would remember the texture of this evening forever and how silly it is to ask God to intervene in conflictual prayers and in prayers in general. It changed my experience of religious life totally. I really didn't give a shit about anyone except Jed and I couldn't prove I cared for him because I was in prison and not sitting at the kitchen table enjoying our bowl of Cheerios together. It was the first tear I shed for a long time and it would be a while before I would shed another.

* * *

I was paroled to a friend's apartment in Milwaukee, WI in November 1987. After giving a clean urine test for thirty days upon my release, I was allowed to move back to Wisconsin Dells to be closer to Jed. While in prison I sent letters to the enclosed megamall in Edmonton, Canada, and researched the tourism pattern in the Dells area. The

Canadian mega-mall was more than 115 football fields under one roof. The first year they opened they had over half a million visitors. In 1985, more than 1.5 million people visited the Dells area each year. Eighty percent of the visitors didn't know they were going to the Dells until Thursday night since the weather was the key factor for those tourists. The number one reason tourists go to the Dells area is for its beauty; any man-made structure would have to compliment the natural beauty of the Dells area. I envisioned a glass dome hundreds of feet in the air covering at least 43 acres. One day I told Jed about my dream and Jed thought the idea was "so cool." Jed and I often talked and visualized the mega dome in the Dells area. On weekends we would search the Dells area for the right location.

"Dad, we better not tell Mom or anyone what we're talking about. They'll never believe us."

"That's true, Jed. We won't tell anyone." After meeting so many people who doubted my dream I realized only a child would talk, visualize, and imagine such a magnificent project.

One day I took a different way back to

BRAIN CHANGE

Jed's house when we saw a for sale sign,

"Forty-three acres for sale by owner," with a number to call.

I rehearsed what I would say and called the number from the sign.

"Hello, Mr. Timm speaking."

"Hi, Mr. Timm. My name is Lyle Wildes and I have a dream. I would like to use some of your land to develop it. Would you be interested in hearing more about my dream?"

Mr. Timm chuckled and asked,

"Where are you calling from?"

"Downtown Dells."

"Have you checked out the property?"

"I drove past it, but I didn't feel comfortable driving on your property."

"Why don't we meet at Perkins Restaurant?" Mr. Timm suggested.

We sat in a large U-shaped corner booth.

"Tell me about your dream, Lyle."

"I want to put a clear dome over a large mass of land and build a city under it. I want to help make Wisconsin Dells a destination as well as a retirement area."

Mr. Timm leaned back and took a deep breath.

BRAIN CHANGE

"That's quite a venture. Do you have access to that kind of money?"

"I don't have it today but when I find the right property, I will get it."

"So you think my property is it?" Mr. Timm asked.

"I think so. It has the right access from the interstate. It's on the outskirts of the Dells yet close enough to utilize the city's services."

Mr. Timm took a sip of his coffee and looked over his glasses.

"How do you intend to generate that much money?"

"I intend to ask those individuals with enough money who are interested in helping develop my dream. Someone who sees the future of the Dells the same way I do. Right now, I need to find the perfect spot and get access to it."

"All you have to do is come up with the money and you can have access to my property."

"I have a unique deal for you to consider."

"I'm not interested. I just want to sell my property."

"Great."

"Well, do we have a deal?"

"What kind of down payment are you looking for?"

"Ten percent."

"I don't have $25,000. Can I make a counter offer?"

"What kind of an offer do you have in mind?" Mr. Timm asked.

"If you will let me give you a small down payment and then give me six months to raise the rest of the money, I will not argue about the price. If I can't generate the money in that period of time, I will give you another small down payment if you agree to extend it for another six months. However, you can increase the price of the property by ten percent after the first six months for giving me additional time, if I need it, to raise the money."

There was a moment of silence. I continued,

"Mr. Timm, you know we will both win if I can put this project together."

"Sure, but I just want to sell my land today."

"Here is my proposal. But before I present it, I would like to ask you a couple of questions."

65

BRAIN CHANGE

"Go for it."

"You had the land listed for about two years now. It seems that the Dells is developing south and not so much this way, to the North. Plus, you have had to pay the taxes on this piece of property each year, right?"

"Yeah . . . but . . ."

"I'll give you $1,000 as a down payment and you give me six months to raise the money."

"You're crazy, Lyle. That's not even one percent. Why would I do that?"

"Because no one is going to buy that property in the next six months."

"How do you know?"

"Do you have any nibbles on the property at this time?"

"Well, no . . ."

"Well then, let me pay some of the taxes and you give me six months to find investors."

"When would I get the $1,000 or do you have to ask someone for that, too?"

"Today, right now. I have $1,005 in my pocket. I even have enough to buy our coffee. I came ready to deal."

Mr. Timm sat back and laughed.

BRAIN CHANGE

"I don't believe you think I would ever consider tying up that much real estate with only a $1,000 down."

"Mr. Timm, the deal gets better."

"Really? How much better?"

"If I haven't generated the necessary funds in six months you can keep the $1,000 and I'll give you an additional $500 and you can increase the price by ten percent. But then I ask that you give me an additional six months. At the most, this would give me a full year to find investors. If I don't generate the money in that length of time, the property goes back to you and you keep the $1,500 dollars."

Mr. Timm got up from the booth.

"I'll have to talk it over with my wife before I can give you an answer."

"That's fine, but let me give you the $1,000 today and you give me a receipt. If your wife doesn't object, then we can draw up the papers later this week. Would that be okay?"

After a moment of silence, Mr. Timm looked at me and said,

"You're really persistent, aren't you? Alright, I'll give you a receipt but I still have to talk it over with my wife."

BRAIN CHANGE

A few days later Mr. Timm called.

"My wife's on your side, Lyle. We have the papers ready to sign. You want to stop by our house?"

"No, let's meet on the property."

Mr. Timm, his wife, and I met to sign the papers on the hood of Mr. Timm's pickup. After I signed the papers I asked,

"Would you be interested in hearing about another good offer?"

"An offer on what?" Mr. Timm asked.

"There's a beautiful home on Rocky Arbor Lake. Do you own it, too?"

"Yes, we have it listed. Our renters left last fall and we haven't been able to rent it, but once school begins again this fall, we anticipate renting it to a school teacher."

"How much are you asking for rent?"

"We have been collecting $650 per month."

"May I make an offer?"

"What's on your mind, Lyle?"

"Well, since I'm going to be looking for exclusive investors, I should have a nice house to meet them in, don't you agree? I will move thousands of dollars worth of nice furniture into your house and pay you $350 per month, starting a month from today.

I'll agree to rent it for one year. If I haven't lived up to my agreement with the land, I will move out and leave you a house full of expensive furniture."

Mr. Timm backed away from the front of his pickup.

"I'll be crazy to do it at that price."

"But Jimmy," his wife said. "We haven't had any income from it for over a year now. At least someone would be living in it and we would have $350 per month to pay the taxes and put the rest on our loan payment."

"Honey, whose side are you on? You're not saying we should rent our property for that, are you?"

"If Lyle doesn't live up to his agreement, we would have a house full of nice furniture."

Mrs. Timm continued,

"Besides, it would probably rent faster with nice furniture. It seems Lyle is willing to risk everything. Remember when you had your dream, honey? We should at least give Lyle a chance."

"What kind of furniture do you have?"

"I have cork lamps, brass and glass end tables, a beautiful kitchen set, china hutch, an elegant bedroom set, and a very nice love seat and sofa."

"Where is the furniture?"

"In a warehouse in Lodi, Wisconsin. We can go look at it right now, if you want."

Mr. Timm sighed and looked at his wife.

"No, that won't be necessary."

"Good. You write up the agreement and I'll go get the furniture. If you give me the key today, I will have the furniture arranged when you come over and can see the furnishings. Do we have a deal?"

"Let's do it, Jimmy," said Mrs. Timm.

Mr. Timm stood for a while.

"I think this hot sun has affected our thinking, honey. I don't believe we're renting our home on the lake for $350 per month without any cash up front or even a security deposit. Have we gone crazy?"

"Can I have your attention for just a moment?"

I walked around the truck so I was standing between Mr. Timm and his wife.

"Listen, folks. I'm not a con man but rather a man with a dream in which I am willing to put everything on the line for this opportunity to succeed. If I can't generate the money needed to pay off this property and home, how will I ever be able to generate hundreds of millions to develop my dream?

BRAIN CHANGE

All I'm asking for is this one opportunity. If you work with me on this, I'll give you my word that I will never take advantage of your kindness, compassion, and good business sense."

"What good business sense?" Mr. Timm asked.

"Do we have a deal?"

Mrs. Timm put her arm around her husband. "What do you think, honey? Let's give Lyle a chance to build his dream."

"Lyle, do you promise not to cause us any problems? We really don't want to get involved in anything negative at this time in our lives. Will you promise us that?"

"I assure you, folks, that if I fail I will leave without any problems to you."

"That's good," Mr. Timm said. "We're going to trust you. The land and house is yours for one year."

* * *

I tied up the land and home to develop this idea to change the experience at Wisconsin Dells. I was also introduced to a wonderful woman, Lynne, by her bother whom I had met in the Fox Lake prison facility. Lynne was spending a lot of time with me in the Dells. She liked the area. She subtly asked questions that went over my head, questions like,

"Lyle, do you really like that waterbed of yours?"

Little did I know she was thinking about sleeping with me long-term, but not on that waterbed. Lynne knew I was looking for hundreds of thousands of dollars and I think she was wondering about my ability to face reality. Lynne started to come up to the Dells on weekends because I was working on my major project there. We were still building our relationship when Lynne hinted that if I asked her properly she might want to move to the Dells. I asked Lynne to marry me and she agreed. She agreed to move to Wisconsin Dells and we planned our wedding for June 10, 1989. We would live in this neat home on the man-made Rocky Arbor lake north of Wisconsin Dells.

* * *

Two weeks before the six-month deadline I got an appointment with Jack and Bob Van Metre, two highly respected investors in Madison, WI. I rented a stretched white limousine. They brought John Gresens, another potential investor and a friend of mine. These three gentlemen didn't know my deadline was two weeks away. As the limo pulled away I said,

"I want to thank all of you for taking the time to come and look at this land with me. This is one of the most beautiful parts of the Dells. This is going to be a really special day for all of us."

"Okay, Wildes," said John. "It's time you tell us what you're really up to in the Dells."

"The reason I wanted you to come is . . . the Dells is in need of transition and we will be the ones to initiate that transition."

"What's the transition?" Jack asked.

"My research tells me that sixty percent of the people who end up in the Dells on Friday did not know they were going to go Thursday."

"And why is that?" Bob asked.

"That's because weather is a major factor in people going to the Dells. There's no place for them to go when it rains."

I spoke into the limo intercom:

"Please take exit 92 through the Dells."

Then, to the three gentlemen:

"I'm going to show you what I'm talking about."

The exit led to the main avenue through the Dells. The men watched through the windows at outdoor water slides, bumper cars, miniature golf, roller coasters, horses, and open faced stores all nearly closed down. It was raining, and there were very few people in the Dells.

"See how no one is outside? On a sunny day there would be thousands of people at each event."

"So what are you going to do about that?" Bob asked.

"I want to put all of these key things under one huge roof on the piece of property we are looking at today."

"How much do you think this would cost?" Bob asked.

"More than $500 million."

"Isn't that an awful lot of money to spend in the Dells? No one else is spending that much in the Dells," Bob noted.

"That's because no one else has noticed the potential of the Dells. Tommy Bartlett told me that anyone who spends more than five million in the Dells will go broke. He said the Dells can't support it. I told him, 'No disrespect, Mr. Bartlett, but that's old thinking.'"

"So what makes you think this will work?" John asked.

"They built one of these in Edmonton, Canada, hoping to get 400,000 people to come to that desolate town. The first year they got 900,000 because weather was the controlling factor. Just imagine, the Dells is attracting a very small portion of the market. Within one tank of gas from the Dells there are more than 30 million potential customers and only 1.5 million came last year."

I again spoke into the intercom:

"Please turn on Highway H and take a right on Old Sauk Road."

"So this is the property we're looking at?" John asked.

"Yes. This is the beginning of it."

"Please turn right at the entrance into the hayfield camouflaged by low hanging branches and thick leaves."

The rain had stopped but the grass was slippery and wet. After a few minutes of standing in awe in the midst of trees, birds chirping, crickets, and frogs croaking the investors agreed it was a beautiful piece of property. They finished their cigarettes and started walking back toward the limo. I knew if their interest ended they would never invest in the property.

"Hold on, gentlemen. We're going to take a walk down this ledge to the cliffs below that overlook an awesome valley."

They laughed.

"Some other time, Lyle, but not today."

"You know how difficult it was to arrange a time when all four of us could get together?" I said. "We must do it today."

"Why?"

"Because . . . you must experience the wonder, beauty, and peace that reside in the midst of these trees and cliffs. The beauty of the Dells is the number one reason why so many people come here. And now I want you to experience it with me. If you aren't overcome by this experience, I will pay for dry cleaning your clothes."

"I am wearing an expensive suit and a costly pair of wing-tips. You don't expect me to climb down into that wet, tangled mess dressed like this, do you?" Jack asked.

"Yes I do, gentlemen. You should have come dressed for such an event. After all, that is why we came up here. Right?"

BRAIN CHANGE

"Okay, how do we get down there?" Bob asked.

"Just follow me, gentlemen."

As John lit another cigarette he said,

"I'm staying up here. Someone has to call a doctor in case someone has a heart attack."

Everyone laughed. Jack, Bob, and I trekked down the hillside to the cliffs. We moved down the tree-covered hillside and saw squirrels and beautiful birds, and a rabbit scampering off. We descended deeper into the plush rich forest of rural South Central Wisconsin. We clung to bushes, twigs, and small limbs to keep from falling down the hillside.

They reached the sheer cliffs overlooking an old river bed. The investors were in awe by its beauty. The sound of frogs, birds, and other wildlife was a natural symphony to the magnificence of the sandstone cliffs. There was a majestic island centered in the middle of the riverbed with one huge pine tree standing as if a sentry on guard. It was a moment of pure wonder. I thought,

"Yes, it is happening. These men are caught in the beauty, wonder, and peace that surfaced in the midst of this moment of pure nature." It was a moment when nothing else mattered.

"I would love to stay here all day, it is so peaceful," Jack said.

"How are we ever going to get back up out of here?" Bob asked.

"Don't worry, men. There's a trail out over here."

"Why didn't we come that way in the first place?" Bob asked.

"If we had come in the other way, you would have missed all this beauty."

Climbing back up out of the forest, the investors looked like they had lost a major battle. Their shoes were covered with mud and burrs were stuck everywhere but they were transformed by being in the midst of such beauty. Jack and Bob complained as they picked off hundreds of burrs. They climbed back into the limo and we drove off the property.

"Let's see this house on the lake you rented, Lyle," John said.

When the stretched white limousine pulled into my driveway, every curtain flew back in my neighbors houses. My investors liked the place and while sitting on the deck I offered to fix them a drink. They sat there in the midst of towering pines with birds singing and the sun reflecting off the surface of the small lake. No one said a word for some time until Bob asked,

"Lyle, can we meet with the realtor today?"

I walked into the house and called Mr. Timm. Fortunately, he answered.

"Mr. Timm, my investors are asking to meet with you."

"When?" he asked

"Now."

"Now? Today? Where?"

"At the Brother-In-Laws Tavern on the main avenue in downtown Dells."

It felt like I was in a movie. When Mr. Timm arrived, Jack said,

"We're interested in the forty-three acres you have for sale through Lyle. How much do you want for it today?"

"Well, you know what I'm asking for it," said Mr. Timm.

"You give me your final price and we'll say yes or no," said Jack.

Mr. Timm looked at me in disbelief, then back at Jack and asked,

"When would you be paying for this?"

"We'll give you a check today."

Mr. Timm pulled a pen from his pocket, wrote out a number and slid the paper across the table. Jack looked at Bob and said,

"I think we have a deal."

Bob pulled a checkbook out of his inside coat pocket and wrote the full amount to Mr. Timm. After handing him the check Bob asked,

"How much is the house Lyle's renting from you?"

Mr. Timm looked perplexed.

"Are you serious?"

"Just give us your bottom number, Mr. Timm."

Mr. Timm wrote another number on a piece of paper and another check was cut.

"Have we bought enough property for your project now, Lyle?" asked Jack.

"Yes, sir. Thank you very much."

"Well, we've got everything done here. Let's go," said John.

We drank champagne in the limo on the way back to Madison. Jack and Bob didn't use drugs, so John and I dropped them off before celebrating the miracle and mystery of life that took place in Wisconsin Dells.

* * *

BRAIN CHANGE

I was working on the project in the Dells when John introduced me to a friend of his to make some quick money. His friend was bringing some good coke into Madison. The night of our deal dragged out until the connection called and asked me to meet him at the Shamrock Bar in Madison. As I sat waiting at the bar I noticed people coming in I had never seen before. My gut told me there was trouble but my greed overrode it. The connection arrived dressed in a new jogging suit (unknown by me, wired up) and asked me to follow him into the bathroom. I insisted we go down to my office on Doty Street. He refused so I followed him like a sheep to the slaughterhouse. We entered the bathroom at 9:00 pm on May 24, 1989, when he jammed a small box into my stomach and clearly stated on tape,

"Here are your drugs, man."

I didn't take the box but looked up at him and asked,

"What the fuck are you doing?"

The bathroom door crashed open with officers yelling,

"Put your hands up. You're under arrest!"

BRAIN CHANGE

I knew I had just been set up, but by whom? A badge came flying over my head and landed in the sink in front of me. Then a gun flew into the sink as one officer started yelling,

"My gun. He's got my gun."

I was grabbed and taken off to the Dane County Jail. I used my one phone call to call Lynne. I was supposed to be home earlier in the evening and now it was the next day. I heard her sadly say,

"Hello?"

"Hi, Lynne"

"Hi, Lyle. What are you doing? Why aren't you home?"

"I'm in jail, Lynne."

"It's not for drugs, is it, Lyle?"

"It is, Lynne. They tell me I have an arraignment tomorrow and I'll find out what is going on then."

I was denied bond and had to remain in jail until my case went to trial, which I lost. This time I was found guilty of a conspiracy to purchase a controlled substance with intent to deliver cocaine. There were no drugs in the box, and I was one of the first cases for a reverse buy to be tested as a legal practice in the drug war. Because of my past prior two felonies, I was considered a career offender and required level thirty-two on the matrix of the new sentencing guidelines. I could receive a sentence between 20 and 25 years. I was given two hundred and sixty four months by Judge Shabazz. I can still see my attorney calculating out the months on a piece of paper equaling twenty-two years.

Needless to say, my wedding with Lynne never took place and my project in the Dells was cancelled. Before I began my journey to the Metropolitan Correctional Center (MCC) in Chicago, Lynne came to visit me in the Madison Dane County Jail. I can remember it happening as if it was yesterday. Lynne picked up the intercom phone and stoically asked me to place my hands against the thick glass which separated us. I thought I could feel the warmth of her hands as she stood there with the phone cradled on her shoulder.

"Lyle, I came here today to tell you that I love you, but . . . I put my hands in yours and you dropped them. I put my heart in your care and you broke it. I bought into your hopes and dreams and you shattered them all. I am moving on. Best of luck to you, Lyle."

BRAIN CHANGE

As I took in her words my arms felt heavy and my legs felt like rubber. My stomach tightened and I felt cold, lost, helpless. She relocated the phone in its cradle and pushed the button to be released. She then kissed the palm of her left hand and blew a final kiss my way. This was the second time since my accident I shed any tears. I didn't feel her pain as I did Jed's; this time I only felt mine. Our relationship lasted only eighteen months but I had the wonderful experience of meeting this great woman, Lynne.

Sitting on my bunk in county jail I saw for the first time how the naked reality of my actions clearly caused this chaos. I was about to start my journey alone into the Federal Bureau of Prisons.

20 years locked up...

"Lyle, you will have to blossom where you are planted."

- Fr. Clair Dinger
Milan Prison Chaplain

I was bussed to the Chicago MCC, where I was designated to the Milan, MI, medium security prison. From Chicago I was moved to Terre Haute, IN, a hub for moving federal prisoners to their designated facilities. From there I was flown by Con Air, Bureau Of Prison's (BOP) airplane, to Detroit, MI, and then bussed from the airport to the Milan federal prison where I remained for over eight years. The Milan prison had rumors of imprisoning Helen Gillis, wife of Baby Face Nelson, and Evelyn Frechette, wife of John Dillinger, both when it was a woman's facility.

The BOP bus driver parked the bus tight up against the prison entrance wall.

BRAIN CHANGE

Guards flanked in a half-circle behind the bus; a number of pickups pulled up behind the standing guards holding their weapons and anxious dogs. The guard in the gun tower could see for miles in every direction to detect any approaching escape attempts. Sitting in the bus waiting to be moved onto the compound I felt alone, detached from everything and everybody. About thirty of us were moved from the bus to a holding tank inside the prison compound where there was standing-room only. As we waited for our name to be called, an elderly man believed he wasn't getting enough oxygen. He was about to fall out when one of the other prisoners pointed to a plastic window in front of me with holes drilled in it. The man worked his way over to the window and drew in what he thought was fresh air. I didn't like his intrusion since I was in this unique spot giving me access to the fresh air. After he had relaxed and was feeling normal one of the more outspoken prisoners laughed and pointed to the recovering man.

"Look at that fool. He thinks he's getting fresh air, but there's another window behind it sealing it off. I told you it was all in your head. Now look at you, all better because you thought you found fresh air when it's the same old air. That's fucked up, buddy."

I thought I had access to fresh air when, in fact I, too, was breathing the same old air.

* * *

Every new arrival on each prison compound has to attend an Admission & Orientation (A&O) session. Everyone in federal prison, including the handicapped, have to find a job. If you don't find a job within a couple of weeks after attending A&O you're assigned to the dish room, or hell, as it is known by some inmates. I recalled meeting Bill when I was back in MCC Chicago who encouraged me to work as a chapel clerk, his own job, since he was going to be released soon. When I left MCC he said he would talk to the Chaplain for me. I was scheduled to attend A&O where the head of each department informs the new arrivals of the services they provide and any jobs available in their department. Fr. Dinger, Head of Religious Services presented the second day and when his segment was over I approached him and asked,

"Excuse me, Father. Did your clerk, Bill,

talk to you about hiring me?"

"What's your name?"

"Lyle Wildes."

"Oh, yes. Check the call-out sheet for tomorrow."

The next day I was on the call-out sheet to be interviewed by Fr. Dinger. After my interview he said he would let me know. Worried about not hearing from Fr. Dinger, I plotted ways to get Fr. to hire me. I knew how the underground economy worked in state prison; I decided to buy a bag of coffee, some cookies, and a few protein bars in hopes Bill could hurry Fr. Dinger's decision along. A couple of days following my donation to Bill, I was on the change sheet from A&O status to the Chapel. I was now Fr. Dinger's orderly. I will never know if it was because of the cookies or if Fr. simply decided to hire me. I was hired as an orderly and my job was to keep the floor polished. After a couple of months working as an orderly Fr. asked me to check out the floors with him. He asked me if I noticed anything different about the chapel library floor.

"It is not as shiny as it used to be."

"Yes, that is right. I do not believe you are the man for the orderly job. I am going to move you into the clerk's office as my chapel clerk."

I was relieved because I thought I was going to get fired from a prison job and it's nearly impossible to get fired as an inmate. I loved working as a chapel clerk and worked many hours for the other clerks. It gave me quiet time to read and type.

* * *

Soon after beginning my career as a chapel clerk, I noticed a flier on the wall asking prisoners to sign up for a Positive Mental Attitude (PMA) class taught by an inmate. I knew of the inmate from his involvement in the Protestant Sunday morning services. Twelve of us signed up for the first PMA class. Upon completing the twenty-week class, I was asked if I would like to co-facilitate the next class. I decided to take the offer. The first class focused on beginning a new life, even in prison. We talked about the learning process and how we acquire many of our values and beliefs from our caregivers. For some reason, the story about Jed experiencing a violent storm came to my mind.

"I have never thought about this special moment with Jed until co-facilitating this class. After my auto accident I ended my eight-month marriage by getting a divorce. My parents said I was not the son they raised and disowned me. When they told me they were disowning me, I decided to have a vasectomy so they would never be able to enjoy any grandchildren from me. Some ten years later, I became connected to my significant other's nine-month-old baby. I have no idea why that happened since I was known for not caring about anyone, especially kids.

"One day I came home as the sky was getting black and the wind was blowing branches off the trees in our yard. I entered the house, and this little helpless person came running across the floor as if wondering what was happening outside. I picked him up and carried him to the back door where his mom was finishing up in her rose garden. As we were talking about the storm, her safety, and the flying debris, lightning cracked on the backside of our house. Immediately, thunder shook the house and rattled the windows. While holding Jed in my arms, he turned and grabbed my beard pulling us face to face as if asking,

'What's happening, Da-da?'

"I waved my right hand across the sky and said,

'Beautiful, Jed. Beautifullll.'

"Jed released my beard and pointed at the sky and screamed,

'Oooooooo.'

"The lightening continued to split the evening sky and thunder filled the air.

"A few years later while at a friend's house another storm was developing. This time my friend's daughter, who was Jed's age, pulled Jed into her bedroom and demanded,

'We have to get under the bed, Jed.'

"Jed was confused and asked,

'Why?'

'The storm can hurt us. We must get under my bed to be safe.'

"I then realized her Dad curses storms and yells,

'I hate these damn storms. One day it will blow our house over.'

"Telling this story today, I realize how Jed caught an appreciation for storms and my friend's daughter caught a fear of storms. Our kids simply catch the values and beliefs of their caregivers. When I was still communicating with Jed's mother I asked if she noticed anything special about Jed and storms.

'Well, he sits in the window seat and pulls the curtains open and watches the storms.'

'He isn't afraid?' I asked.

'No. He loves to watch what he calls the light show.'"

* * *

In one of the PMA classes we talked about increasing our value in the marketplace. I told my experience of working in the local Reedsburg Bank. A banking representative from the local Reedsburg Bank came to our high school looking for a young man who wanted to become a banker. I was interviewed and offered the opportunity to start a banking career during my senior year. Mom wanted me to go to college but was excited about this opportunity, while Dad clearly thought it was a sissy's job. I suddenly felt "In-Between" from being a hard-working farm boy and construction worker and becoming a banker. This was a

BRAIN CHANGE

huge change in my life, and I had no plan in place to help me make the transition. I clearly felt In-Between. I didn't move into Reedsburg or consider the importance of asking my family for permission to become a banker. As a result, I failed mentally to make the transition.

Each evening when I arrived back to the farm my dad would harass me. He commented about how my hands were starting to look like a sissy's. My brain had felt approval through hard physical labor. My parents, friends and neighbors looked up to me because of my physical abilities. My new job offered approval through communication skills, public image, and mental acuity. I had not practiced those needed skills, causing me to slowly dislike my new job. I had no process for making the transition during this feeling In-Between.

Don Proper, the president of the bank, overlooked my growing conflict with these two worlds. He loved being a banker and thought anyone would enjoy living the banking lifestyle. This joy would spur a quick learning of the banking world's vocabulary. Little did I or anyone else realize the need to coach my brain through the process

BRAIN CHANGE

of letting go of one world and accepting another. I needed to coach my brain to accept the different values and beliefs of a banker. Without coaching my brain through this In-Between time, I sabotaged my banking opportunity and clearly defaulted to those values and beliefs of a farm boy. My brain lived and developed the lifestyle of a small farm, and suddenly walking into a banker lifestyle made me feel out of place, uncomfortable, and anxious. Not acknowledging and unable to process this feeling of being In-Between kept me out of the banking industry. After working in the bank a year and a half I walked into Mr. Proper's office and told him I was quitting my job. He was shocked that I didn't want to be a banker. By now I couldn't understand why anyone except a bunch of soft pear-shaped men would want to be a banker. My brain's neurological network supporting my invisible farm boy values and beliefs caused me to sabotage this banking opportunity. When I told my mother I had quit my banking job, she had mixed feelings. When I told Dad, he was happy and assumed I would want to return to working the farm and doing construction work.

My brain outlasted and resisted the

effort I made to coach it into becoming a banker. My brain's resistance was greater than the little brain coaching done to get it through this transitional period. Not knowing how to coach my brain through this transition kept me from becoming a banker. I suppose that many have sabotaged an opportunity because they didn't know how to coach their brain through the mental transition or the period of In-Between. Knowing how to coach one's brain can free anyone of their neurological prison, often locked tighter than any prison gate.

* * *

Everyone probably has felt In-Between at some time in their life. For me, feeling In-Between was a way of life before and during my incarceration. Because my time in state prison was so short I did not experience this feeling of In-Between. I was in and out so quickly I only felt an interruption and not a change in lifestyle. My federal period of incarceration was for twenty-two years under the New Law, meaning I would be incarcerated for two decades. In 1987, Congress created what is referred

BRAIN CHANGE

to as the New Law, requiring offenders to serve 87.5% of their sentence. Prior to the New Law you were eligible for discretionary parole after serving 25% of your sentence. The old sentencing structure was not seen as tough on crime so Congress eliminated discretionary parole for federal prisoners. This would mean each prisoner would serve a lot more time before being released, creating a new concern about the prisoner's reentry process.

Because of the New Law and the length of my sentence, I have identified three stages in the process of incarceration: 1) start of incarceration; 2) heart of incarceration; and 3) tail-end of incarceration. After lengthy periods of incarceration, one who is approaching reentry experiences a strong feeling of being "In-Between" the learned incarceration lifestyle and the unfamiliar, post incarceration lifestyle. Many who have done long periods of time come out of prison frozen at the age of their arrest.

In-Between my lifestyle prior to my incarceration and learning my new prison lifestyle is when I met Fr. Dinger. He coached me to accept a positive perspective of incarceration while working as his prison

Chapel Clerk. While processing this transition of becoming a prisoner and a chapel clerk, Fr. spent a lot of time discussing and sharing ideas about my new lifestyle. He said I would now be living with inmates from fifty different countries on the Milan compound. There were twenty-one different religions being practiced each week in rooms around our offices. Fr. slowly stretched my thinking, making smooth my transition from society to prison life and then being a chapel clerk. His first physical action was handing me a book and asking me to read fifty pages of it each day. It was a hardback book with lots of pages and no pictures. It was *Dark Night of the Soul* by Saint John of the Cross.

"I haven't read a book like this in years."

"I'm only asking you to read fifty pages a day."

"Well, I do have a little extra time on my hands. I suppose I could give it a try."

The author and I had imprisonment in common, but we viewed our incarceration differently. Saint John of the Cross saw his experience as an opportunity to get closer to God, and I viewed my experience as a debilitating punishment. After handing me the book, Fr. Dinger spoke these powerful words.

"Lyle, St. John believed he could find fertile soil in his prison lifestyle, allowing him to blossom where he was planted. You are now planted for many years in a prison environment and I do not want you to wilt and mentally starve because you don't believe there is fertile soil in your prison experience."

I left his office thinking Fr. Dinger was crazy. I could not see any fertile soil in this experience.

* * *

Early in my incarceration, Tony Puttman, a practicing Siddha Yoga leader, called Fr. Dinger out of the blue and asked if any men in prison would be interested in practicing Siddha Yoga Meditation. I now attribute this as a gift out of the mystery of life. When Fr. mentioned it to me I talked with men who were watching various religious videos to learn spiritual alternatives. Six of us signed up to learn about meditation. Before the first class, I was able to do some research on meditation. I found more than 2,000 studies were conducted in 400 universities over the past 40 years. They have consistently demonstrated many positive benefits. When the six of us showed up for our first meditation experience, Tony told us he had been practicing Siddha Yoga since Baba Muktananda came to the United State to introduce Siddha Yoga to America in 1979. The word Yoga means yoking together the mind and body. We did not do any physical yoga movements but simply sat quietly and focused on our breathing, quieting our inner thoughts. He instructed us to place our feet flat on the floor and sit up straight but not rigid.

"Close your eyes and focus on your breath coming in and going out."

As we sat silent, a few seconds felt like it was never going to end. I found my attention bouncing to every new sound and various inner thought. I often had to bring my focus back to my breath as it would quickly fade off again and again. What seemed like an hour was less than a minute. Tony broke the silence by gently asking us to bring our attention back to the room. He invited us to open our eyes and be present when we were ready. Giving us a moment to be present, he then asked if anyone lost focus on their breath. We all raised our hands and laughed.

"Think how hard it was to remain focused on your breath in this quiet room. Now picture how difficult it is to quiet your brain or thoughts when you're angry. It takes practice and that is what we will be doing each week."

There are many names for meditation; *mindfulness* and *being in the present moment* are both common. Throughout this book, I will refer to this practice as *quieting the brain*. I believe we must start a new language for understanding our brain, overriding the repetitive inner chatter. Our brain's chatter subtly overrides our focus so gently we simply don't notice it happening. When we observe our loss of focus, we have to intentionally bring our attention back to our breath. This exercise revealed to me I am not my brain and therefore I am able to interrupt my brain's chatter and quiet it down. Not being my brain means I can, and must, coach my own brain. This also means that if I don't coach my brain someone else will. Years ago, my brother suggested I monitor my brain after having a drink or two. If I don't, he told me, my brain will think I am much smarter and tougher than I really am. I began to believe a new life was possible if I could coach my brain and override the brain's inner chatter. Now, I have to ask myself,

"Who is this 'I or me' capable of monitoring, coaching, and quieting my brain?"

* * *

While working as the chapel clerk and co-facilitating the Positive Mental Attitude (PMA) class I was called to the UNICOR (Federal Prison Industries) office and offered a job. I could make about two hundred and fifty dollars per month and save a couple hundred dollars each month during my incarceration. Over the next 10 years at Milan I could accumulate roughly twenty thousand dollars. I knew it was possible because I heard other men talking about the money they were saving while working at UNICOR. There was one catch: I couldn't teach the PMA class and I would have to give up my chapel clerk's job. Since I didn't have any outstanding fines it was unlikely that the staff would force me to work for UNICOR.

I told Fr. Dinger about my offer and he

seemed disappointed about my leaving the chapel, even though I wasn't active in any religion. Fr. Dinger simply said,

"Lyle, you have to blossom where you're planted."

I asked,

"Blossom in prison? What the hell are you talking about?"

"There is fertile soil and sunlight in every environment, even prison. You just have to find it, Lyle."

I walked out of his office and went back to my unit. The next morning I went back to work and told Fr.,

"I don't know what to do about UNICOR."

Fr. just smiled and asked,

"Are you sure you're asking the right question?"

"What do you mean?"

"Why don't you ask what kind of a man do you want to BE instead of asking what you should DO? If you know what kind of a person you want to BE, you'll know what you have to DO, and that will tell you what you'll HAVE."

We sat there in silence until Fr. added,

"Do you want to make bomb racks to

carry bombs or do you want to help others live a better life? That's the question before you today."

Fr. sat in his office and looked at the floor as I processed what he had just shared. Fr. continued,

"What do you value, Lyle? Is it helping the men here in prison or acquiring money?"

"I really enjoy our conversations and I also enjoy facilitating the PMA class. I'm sure my experience would be different working for UNICOR."

I looked at Fr. Dinger and saw something I really respected.

"I'm going to stay here with you, Fr., and help the men in whatever ways I can."

Fr. Dinger responded,

"Well, everyone has a cross to bear and I guess you're mine until I retire. However, this may cause me to retire early."

Then he smiled his seldom-seen smile.

"Okay, Lyle. Get back to your hole in the wall and get to work, whatever it is you do there."

* * *

In 1990, the Seventh Circuit Court

of Appeals affirmed my twenty-two year conviction (F2d 910, 1484), causing my inner chatter to become hijacked. I was now going to be incarcerated for nearly two decades and my thoughts got away from me. My pulse averaged 101 beats per minute for weeks. One Monday morning while eating breakfast I felt the chow hall begin to shake. I thought an earthquake was happening at Milan, shaking me out of my seat. I reached across the aisle toward a table to balance myself when I felt another prisoner grab my wrist and say, as he threw my hand back to me,

"Hey dude, you better get your life in order or you're going to die before you get out of this fucking hole."

I suddenly realized the earthquake was taking place inside my skin. I thought,

"Wow, I am in serious trouble. I'm going to die for no medical reason other than stress. I have to figure out why I am so stressed. What is causing me to kill myself from stress? How can I save my life?"

* * *

Mom moved to Lime Ridge, WI, and

BRAIN CHANGE

lived alone after Dad died of a heart attack just four months after retirement. She, too, was living In-Between her life with Dad and the way her life was now going to be. She never dated or built a relationship with another man while living alone in Lime Ridge. Every Saturday morning I called Mom and we discussed ideas and I came to believe that isolating and living alone is risky, either in or out of prison. Living with someone else keeps you in a social relationship and in check when your thinking and actions get too distorted. Dr. Karl S. Kruszelnicki described the process in an article I read in prison.

> "If you plunge a frog into a pan of boiling water, it will immediately jump off the surface. But if you place the frog in a pan of cool water and slowly heat it to boiling, the frog doesn't notice the changing temperature and will slowly cook to death before realizing it should jump out."

The frog story reveals how people filter out trouble until it is too late. This process of gradual change was happening to my mother and she was eventually being cooked by her own negative self-talk. This process started when a neighbor lady asked mom in a grocery store how she dealt earlier with her husband's affair. Mom was shocked by her question. The lady realized Mom didn't know about it and apologized as she moved on. The lady's question turned on the heat and Mom's self-talk was the fuel. Mom went home and discussed this matter inside her own head. Her self-talk imagined times Dad could have had an affair. It was easy to recall instances and suspicion fell in place once the heat was on.

One Saturday during one of our phone calls Mom asked,

"Do you think Dad ever had an affair during our marriage?"

I was shocked by her question.

"I do not. Dad was not that kind of a man."

Mom was quick to repeat one of her sayings.

"Ooh. Still water runs deep. Don't ever forget that, Lyle."

"I assure you, Mom. Dad never had an affair."

"How can you be so sure?"

"Dad often acknowledged to me, 'If it wasn't for all the work Mom does, especially in our garden, we wouldn't have all those fresh vegetables to eat. She works longer and harder in the hot sun than any of us. She does that all for us, Lyle.'

"Mom, that was as close as Dad could come to saying he loves you and would never betray you."

Mom couldn't let it go and I quickly learned one negative thought never lives in the brain alone for long. Its negative friends come in and then a family of negative thoughts come in and finally a negative community lives there. The majority of Mom's thoughts were negative. Her thinking turned negative toward the man she loved, then an unknown woman, then my prosecutor, my judge . . . and the list just kept growing. She created a distrustful, hurtful world. I finally had to tell Mom,

"If you keep hating more and more people I'm not going to call you anymore. Negative thinking is caught faster than it can be taught, Mom. You have slowly transformed your own life perspective into a negative mess."

"I don't know what to do, Lyle."

"Mom, write on a sheet of paper the things that make you mad about Dad."

"It would take more than one sheet of paper, Lyle."

I couldn't believe how quickly the woman who was always telling me to be positive and never say life is awful is the same woman on the phone with me now.

"Mom, it doesn't matter how many pages it takes. Just list everything and I'll call you next Saturday."

"Okay."

When I called next Saturday I asked if she had listed everything.

"Yep!"

"Okay, Mom. Here's what I want you to do. Take the list of Dad's violations up to his grave site and dig a small hole on top of his grave. Place those papers in that hole. Light the papers on fire and stand back and watch the smoke carry those violations out of your sight. Then, if you let go, they will be out of your thoughts. Exhale and release them from your memory. Make it a ceremony, okay Mom?"

"Okay," she said, hesitant.

Next Saturday I called again,

"Did you go to Dad's grave?"

BRAIN CHANGE

"I did."

"Did you release all those violations from your self-talk and memory?"

"I think so."

When she said, 'I think so,' I knew she hadn't let go. She didn't mention Dad having an affair for weeks but then, out of the blue, it came up again. I was sad when Mom said she couldn't let go and be the positive person I knew her to be for years.

One day I asked,

"Why couldn't you let go, Mom?"

"Honey, I tried. I really tried."

She begin to cry.

"Lyle, I had nothing to replace those thoughts. They had consumed so much of my thinking. I tried to think about something else, but those thoughts kept crashing back stronger and louder. I thought they must be true, if they wouldn't quiet down."

I realized Mom's brain was locked tighter than my prison cell door. This all happened so slowly. Mom became cooked and would die before she could turn off her own destructive thinking. Mom had no process for dealing with her In-Between and she, too, sabotaged her own life.

BRAIN CHANGE

* * *

After reading *Dark Night of the Soul* and seeing how our thinking affects our expectations, I decided to continue reading fifty pages of nonfiction every day of my incarceration. I focused on the best seller lists related to Neurology, Philosophy, and Psychology. In the late 1980's many articles and books were coming out on brain research. Each week, I checked USA Today's best-selling lists and the next book I read was titled *Ageless Body, Timeless Mind* by Deepak Chopra. I shared a quote from his book with the PMA class participants:

> "Our cells are constantly eavesdropping on our thoughts and being changed by them."

When the PMA participants challenged me on that quote, I asked them to imagine going back to their prison cell and taking out a picture of their wife or girlfriend.
"While holding her nearly nude image in your hand, imagine all the wonderful things you've done with her sexually and how much you look forward to being with her again.

Think how much you miss her, how soft her lips are, and how sweet they taste. Imagine the smell of her perfume floating up into your nostrils as she whispers,

'I love you and want you tonight.'

"Now I ask, do you think you would notice any changes in the cells of your body?"

Laughter breaks out in the room as an inmate shouts,

"Hell, yes!"

"But she's not in the room with you," I continued. "You're there alone with only your thoughts of her and yet the cells of your body changed."

"Hey, Lyle. I understand what you're telling us. But it's hard for me to get my head around this crazy brain shit."

* * *

I had been at Milan nearly twenty-four months and lived in units C and F2. I was now being moved to H-unit, a nonsmoking unit and the best on the compound if you're a nonsmoker. When I checked in with the unit officer he told me to move into room #206 on the right. As I was walking out of his office he said,

"Hey inmate, you have an interesting cellie. He doesn't get along well with others."

When I entered room #206 my cellie was lying on the lower bunk. He looked up at me and said,

"You're not gay, are you? These damn gay kids drive me crazy."

His name was Rodney. As I greeted him I notice his clothing lying on the floor by his bunk. His boxers were on top and smeared with what looked like shit. I didn't know what to say. He looked at them and said,

"Sorry. I have a habit of leaving my clothes lying around."

He reached down and picked up his boxers and noticed the smear.

"What the fuck is this? Is that my shit?" First he smears some on his finger and then smells it and finally licks his finger. I nearly lost it. My first thought was,

"What the fuck did I get myself into this time?"

As he pulls his finger out of his mouth he started laughing.

"It's melted Hershey's chocolate. I just wanted to see how you would react."

I ended up being Rodney's cellie for a couple of years and there was never a dull moment. He was either happy or pissed off. Rodney had no middle ground.

* * *

Every Tuesday Fr. Dinger presented to the new prisoners attending Milan's A&O. It became a ritual for me to assist Fr. Dinger during A&O each week. Nothing unusual happened for years until one week Fr. began telling the men about the various religious services they can attend and the holy books they can check out. They were also told about the many volunteers that visit to do special services the Chaplains weren't qualified to do. After giving out all the information Fr. liked to tell the men why he became a prison Chaplain. The men always slumped in their chairs and crossed their arms as if a sermon was coming. Fr. began,

"I don't know any of you here in this room, but I know one thing for sure. You're all good people. I know this from my religious beliefs and it's important you know it, too."

An older black man stood up in the last row and asked,

"Fr., are you saying I'm a good person?"

"Yes."

"Okay, why don't you go tell the judges and prosecutors?"

The room filled with laughter. Fr. replied,

"I wish I could, but I don't have access to them. Anyway, I believe it is more important that I tell you."

The older black man sat down and looked pensive while Fr. continued his presentation. When Fr. finished the elderly black man stood up again and asked,

"Fr., are you really saying I am a good person?"

"Yes. Let me explain why I believe you are a good person. Our bodies generate energy and that energy manifests into our behavior. That behavior becomes either positive or negative actions. It is either helpful or harmful. You are that pure and good energy. You are not your behavior. That is why I believe you are a good person."

The elderly man remained standing and said,

"You are the first person to ever tell me why I'm a good person. My mother wished she would have aborted me and my dad wished he would have masturbated that night. The people in my neighborhood said

BRAIN CHANGE

I was the worst kid on the block. Everyone told me I was a bad person and I believed them. Do you know what bad people do, Padre?

"Yes. They do bad things."

"That's right. If I would have been told I was a good person when I was young, maybe I wouldn't be in prison today."

"That is possible," Fr. noted.

The elderly man stood there with tears rolling down his cheeks as he addresses his fellow prisoners.

"I want to tell the young men here today that many of you can have a different life if you believe you're a good person. The belief I am a good person would have changed my life. I could have done good things. I am now too old and have been sentenced for too long to ever enjoy this good news. Those of you who are young and wise can benefit from this message."

The elderly man sat down, put his elbows on his knees and rested his head in his hands. Fr. concluded,

"Don't ever judge yourself by your behavior. Always think of yourself as pure energy. Sir, you can be a good person in prison, too. Anyone can change their behavior but there is no need to change the good, pure energy that manifests within you. It is refreshed every second of every day."

I watched the elderly man walk out of the room, and I could sense he realized his life would have been different if he had believed he was a good person. It was profound to see him realize so late in his life it could have been different.

I said to myself,

"I am only forty-five years old. I do not have to believe my life is over and that I can't be a good person and enjoy a good life, even in prison. Maybe Fr. is right. There is fertile soil in my prison experience and I can blossom during my incarceration."

I felt refreshed as I approached Fr. and said,

"That was an awesome experience, Fr."

As he walked toward his office with his slight limp I witnessed his seldom seen smile again as he said,

"That is why I am a Chaplain, Lyle."

* * *

Some of the things that happened in my life during my incarceration I felt were the

BRAIN CHANGE

result of the mystery of life and not of my efforts. The following experience was clearly a gift: Steve, a federal prisoner, came into my life as a participant of the PMA class. Steve was raised by wealthy parents as an only child and a graduate from McGill University with a Master's Degree in Psychology. Steve had very poor social skills and was not liked by most prisoners. He was kind but abrasive. Roger, another federal prisoner, was a well published neurologist but not a participant of the PMA class. Roger worked with Dr. Wilder Penfield during the latter's early experimental brain surgeries. Roger wrote over one hundred articles regarding the research he had done on cats' brains. Roger also had poor social skills and was not appreciated on the compound. Steve encouraged me to meet Roger since I was interested in understanding the human brain.

One beautiful Sunday morning I timed my approach on the walking track so I could merge alongside Roger. As we walked I let him know I heard he was a neurologist and I would like to talk with him for a lap or two if that's okay. His face seemed to light up as he agreed to chat. I began,

BRAIN CHANGE

"Steve tells me you are a well published neurologist. I think I had brain damage and I'm very interested in the brain. I have been in prison for about thirty months and have many more years to do. I think I am in prison because I lost my connection and compassion for my community."

During my talks with Roger I learned he liked coffee and Ho Hos. One day I asked Roger, if I provided fresh hot instant coffee and Ho Hos, would he meet with Steve and me on Sunday mornings for a couple of hours. He looked confused by my question. I continued,

"Roger, I believe you have what I need and I have what you would like."

"Really? What's that?

"I need you to share with me your conclusions from your research on the brain and answer some of my questions. You need Ho Hos and coffee as well as a friendly audience to keep your mind fresh. You could share your mind with Steve and me."

Out of life's mystery, Roger and I worked out a plan. I would reserve a room in the chapel area with a chalk board from 9:00 to 11:00 every Sunday morning. I was to provide hot water, instant coffee, hot chocolate mix,

BRAIN CHANGE

and Ho Hos which we considered our bread and wine. Roger was to provide lectures on his brain research. Steve agreed to provide his critical perspective to keep us on track. We met every Sunday morning and called our small group our Neurological Sunday Morning Service. Fr. allowed us to meet as a group since we recognized the mystery of life in our Sunday morning meetings. Fr. considered our group meeting a stretch of the rules for inmate groups, but he allowed it and even attended a few meetings when he could. Roger, as a neurologist, had an interesting perspective on life as a result of his research and personal experiences. His first presentation was on the results of placing a patch over a newborn kitten's eye for six weeks. After removing the patch, the kitten could not see out of that eye. Roger explained that the retina needed the external stimulation to grow a connection to the brain. The kitten's eye did not receive any external stimulation except after removing the patch, at which time the brain's plasticity allowed the kitten's eye to regain sight and develop a connection to the world.

Roger explained how there are windows for the brain's development and if the brain doesn't receive certain stimulation it misses development. Roger was quick to judge many of the men at Milan as having had a concussion or missing certain developmental stages, resulting in having short attention spans, lack of compassion, and other criminal characteristics. When he mentioned concussions and a lack of compassion my ears perked up. The next few Sundays we learned the names of certain areas of the brain and how there is no one area related to behaviors. When asked about an enduring agent or Self, Roger was quick to reply,

"During functional magnetic resonance imaging, or fMRI, we never witnessed a specific area or Self in the brain for decision making. Decisions are made out of a systemic network making up the brain."

Within his lectures, Roger never referred to a Self but he did talk about neurological activities associated with a concept I coined "Sense Of Self" which subjectively feels real yet is suspended in each neural network. We found pictures from the world books in the library and used them to become more familiar with the vocabulary and activity of neurology. The first few words I learned from Roger were plasticity, Sense Of Self, neurological profile or landscape, inhibitors, and excitories. We continued to meet for all the remaining years of Roger's time in prison. Roger's lectures and Steve's critical thinking during our Neurological Sunday Morning Service were gifts directly out of the mystery of life.

* * *

After teaching the PMA classes for years, reading fifty pages of nonfiction every day, and spending nearly two years in my Neurological Sunday Morning Service with Roger and Steve, I was seeing the brain as the single organ of behavior. The brain's developed neurological landscape allowed the brain to run on automatic pilot and resist change. However, the brain has plasticity allowing it to change; it is strong enough to resist change yet weak enough to be changed if it is driven to develop a specific action. I watched prisoners learn to play an instrument for the first time during their incarceration. Some inmates would practice or drive their brain for months to play an instrument and eventually become capable of playing in one of the prison bands. They drove their brains to develop the neurological landscape to habitually play a specific instrument. Change requires that we drive our brains to be rewired or reconstructed through practice. This reconstruction develops new landscapes or profiles to inhibit the brain's old habitual behaviors and create new behaviors. This is why change is not an intellectual process, but a neurological one.

* * *

Being a chapel clerk, I was asked to help organize a Marriage Encounter for Catholic inmates and their wives who wanted to enhance their religious faith and thus their marriages. The couples participating had to be legally married in the Catholic faith. Three married Catholic couples from the local Catholic church helped Fr. Dinger facilitate the Encounter. The Marriage Encounter was held in the prison visiting room and it was my duty to set up the room in a circle formation and assist in providing snacks and drinks. The Encounter started Friday night at 5:00 pm and would end at 8:00 pm. It

BRAIN CHANGE

would restart again on Saturday at 9:00 am and end at 3:00 pm. The wives had visited their husbands in this same room before, but today was going to be different.

This was the first Marriage Encounter scheduled at the Milan facility. To look good, the men pressed their prison clothes and lifted weights for weeks. The prison's dress code required the wives' skirts to be a certain length and their tops were not allowed to reveal any cleavage. The couples could only kiss upon meeting and leaving. Some of the couples held hands as they listened to Fr. Dinger open the Marriage Encounter with a poem. He explained what was going to take place that Friday and Saturday. Fr. talked about the relationship between a couple's strong faith and a healthy marriage. Saturday had many interesting discussions but one discussion stood out for me. It was between an inmate named Robert and his wife, Amy. Robert was from Detroit, MI. He'd been at Milan for nearly a year and he had another four years left of his sentence. Prior to his incarceration, Robert worked for a car manufacturing company in Detroit making a six digit income. A few months before his retirement the company found reasons to let him go. He never told his wife and left for work every morning as if nothing had happened. He drove around the area wondering how he was going to keep everything in place. He decided to rob a bank by simply handing the cashier a note that read,

"I have a gun and am requesting all your money."

He got away with it, his first robbery. A few days later he robbed another bank, then another and another. He got so comfortable robbing banks, he robbed the local bank where he banked. This ended his bank robbing career. I knew Robert prior to the Marriage Encounter through the PMA class. He often talked about his bank robbing career and felt his brain was hijacked because he couldn't remember the experience of robbing any of the banks. During the Marriage Encounter, Robert and Amy talked openly and profoundly for the first time about his criminal activity. She asked Robert,

"Why didn't you tell me you were let go?"

"I didn't want you to know I had been fired."

BRAIN CHANGE

"Why? Didn't you trust me?"

"We had a wonderful lifestyle and I did not want to be the cause of losing it. Our kids were in private schools and I did not want them pulled out of school. I didn't want you or the kids to know I had failed."

Robert had no process for addressing the change that broadsided him. The way he addressed his In-Between of having a job and not having a job caused him to sabotage his new life. As his wife listened, she begin to cry. She leaned over to kiss him on the cheek, took his trembling fingers into her hands and rubbed them as she said,

"Robert, honey, I want you to know I love you and believe in you. Had you talked with me we could have made lifestyle changes. I would have never considered you a failure."

She continued while crying,

"Honey, I never expected you to provide us with such an expensive house or send our kids to an expensive private school. Had you told me, we could have downsized and changed our lifestyle."

His wife sat back and took a deep breath as she continued,

"I know you're difficult to work with

and you're even difficult to live with at times, but that doesn't make you a bad person or a failure. I've often wanted to talk with you about your attitude, but you always shut me down. Now it is out in the open and I want to talk about it. I want to talk about what's enough, Robert. You always wanted us to have a bigger house, a better car, kids in a better school. I didn't marry you for better material things. We had enough in our lives for me and our children. You seemed driven to have more and bigger every year. It is your love, presence, humor, and creativity you offered me and our kids that we valued. So, honey, what is enough for you to feel you are a good provider, father, and husband? Until you can tell me what's enough, you will be driven to chase an undefined goal."

Robert began to cry as he mumbled,

"I don't know what's enough, honey. Lyle asked me that question in our positive attitude class, too. I just don't know the answer."

His wife stood up and pulled Robert up out of his chair and held him. They both were crying as Fr. suggested we take a break. When the program ended, I thought about what is enough material things for me and what non-material things like compassion, humor, empathy, inspiration, and just being present will I offer others? I imagined Fr. saying,

"What kind of a man do you want to BE, Lyle? That will tell you what to Do and what you will Have."

His gentle voice would follow with,

"What you have will always be enough if you know what kind of a person you want to BE."

The next day I talked with Fr. about the power of the brain when it is broadsided with change forcing it to feel In-Between the way Robert lived before he was let go and the post employment lifestyle. Not having a process for coaching his brain, he became hijacked and responded out of the survival mode of fear and anger. When Robert's brain was hijacked it narrowed its focus on every event and thing as being a friend or foe, good or bad. Robert acted to survive, with limited possible options. This narrowing perspective caused him to sabotage his potentially new lifestyle with his family. It also put him in prison and forced him to possibly lose his marriage. After my transfer, I lost track of Robert and Amy.

BRAIN CHANGE

* * *

During one PMA class we used a video, *The Miracle Man*. It's a true story about Morris Goodman having a successful business and a wonderful family prior to crashing his private airplane and breaking his neck in two places. (You can see the complete video on my website.) The doctors said Morris would never talk, walk, or eat on his own again. Morris was persistent; he never accepted the reality of those professionals who doubted in his total recovery. When the doctors told Morris he ought to be more realistic, that he was never going to have total recovery, Morris shot back these powerful words,

> "It's okay for all of you to doubt my recovery, but when I doubt my recovery . . . that's when I'm in trouble."

After watching this video I realized I had the belief I could make a difference in the delivery of mobile homes, change the culture of Wisconsin Dells, and now I

BRAIN CHANGE

believed I could change the culture on this prison compound. Others may doubt me, but if I doubt myself then I am in trouble, too. I set out to help men change their lives in spite of their past problems and negative prison experience. Morris taught me that change or success is a process. This process always leaves you feeling In-Between. There is a period of time between your old life and your new way of life. Morris' video showed me the way we process our In-Between determines the quality of our new life and possibly our longevity. Morris worked hard to recover from his accident; all of us have to work hard to move through change whether we choose it, or it broadsides us, or it simply creeps up on us.

* * *

I formed the habit of calling my mom every Saturday morning while incarcerated. I can't say why, but I was compelled to call her on this one particular Friday. Because it was Friday night, I had to wait in line for nearly an hour to use a phone. When Mom answered, her voice was exceptionally weak.

"Hi, Hon. I'm really happy you called."

"Why are you so happy I called?"

"My doctor says I'm going to die before Monday morning and I wanted to say goodbye to you."

"Geez, Mom, don't joke around like that. You know my fifty-year-old attorney just died in August."

"I know, Son. I'm not joking. My doctor is giving me until Monday. I'm very, very sick."

"Why didn't you tell me sooner, Mom?" I asked with a frightened voice.

"Oh, I didn't want you to worry. I know you're under a lot of pressure these days yourself."

"Mom, we only have 14 more minutes to talk. What does a son talk to his mother about when there are only 14 minutes left?"

"What do you still need to talk about?"

"Oh my God, I am so glad you were my mom."

"I knew you always loved me, Lyle, and I always loved you. Do you remember what I told you each decade when you would ask me for three things you could trust, after I'm gone?"

"Yes. Don't marry a woman you wouldn't kiss right after she had your baby.

Mom, I never understood that."

"Well, when the midwife laid you on my chest, I just wanted your dad to kiss me and tell me he would help me raise you."

"Oh my God, I never knew that, Mom. There's so much I don't know about you. The other two things were, I will one day be an old man and make sure that old man has a lot of good memories."

"That's right."

"Mom, you're going to die and there is so much about you I don't know. Oh Mom, I am so sorry we didn't talk more."

"Forget that. Here is what I want you to remember in order to be happy." I heard her gasping for air as she continued,

"Always remember, everyone you meet is carrying as many problems and difficulties as they can handle. Don't cause anyone any more pain. You've caused so much pain prior to being arrested. It was a relief when you were arrested. You were not the boy we raised. You just didn't care anymore."

"Oh God, Mom. You're brutal tonight."

I suddenly recalled dad saying,

"Dying people never lie."

Mom continued,

"There's a second part to it, Lyle."

BRAIN CHANGE

"Oh no. What's that?"

"If you should be so fortunate as to relieve so much as a feather of someone's pain from their life, they will smile and their joy will spill over into your life. Maybe being in prison and teaching your Positive Attitude class will help you care more about others than you did after your accident."

I checked my watch and saw we only had a couple of minutes left.

"Mom, I am getting overwhelmed. Can we change the subject?"

She whispered,

"Sure, what else do you need to talk about?"

"I am sorry I ended up in prison, Mom. I didn't want to be in prison when you died. I don't want you to come back as a pissed off poltergeist. It's important you die in peace and you leave me alone."

"I am dying peacefully, Son. You see, precious diamonds are created under extremely high pressure. Now, I'm leaving you alone, causing you to experience more pressure. Now it's up to you to find your way through the daily darkness. You're either coming out of the pressure and darkness of prison as a sparkling personality or you will be a shattered, broken, bitter old man."

She grasped for breath as she continued,

"Dad and I planted the seeds of goodness in you and they have been growing in the fertile field of time. When you call, you always mention you're still doing time, the field of fertile soil."

Mom's voice weakened to nearly a whisper as she continued,

"Okay, Son. I'm tired. I am ready to go. Just remember my words and hopefully you will have a sparkling personality when you get out. Our journey is over, Son, and I have given my best. I have nothing left to give you. I have shown you love and given you hope. There nothing more I can leave behind for you. I have to go now."

Silence filled the phone line.

"Mom? Mom?"

Her fumbling with the receiver filled the phone line until she finally got it back in its saddle, filling the phone line now with an empty hum. Wow, Mom is gone forever. As I hung up the phone I took a deep breath, turned around and walked into my new world feeling alone in what Mom called,

"The fertile field of time."

* * *

"The fact is that the huge knot of nerves in our heads has no nerve devoted to monitoring itself. We thus have no direct sensation of actually possessing a brain. We have to take it on faith. And while it is an idea that we all accept as anatomical truth, it almost never enters our consciousness as we think. Thus our philosophies have almost entirely ignored our brains."

- J. Allan Hobson

While living in prison I slowly discovered that most behavior is not a conscious choice. I met thousands of brains and most of them were running on automatic pilot. They acted out of their learned values and beliefs which seemed to be supported by a neurological landscape. When Tony asked us to monitor or quiet the chatter in our brains, I personally witnessed my brain wanting to run on automatic pilot. When my brain resisted this state of quietness, I realized something special about quieting the brain. I wondered about the relationship between the brain and the Sense Of Self, and the latter's power to override the brain. Brain research does not acknowledge an enduring agent or what we call "I, ME or SELF." Am I only a subjective Sense Of Self dependent on the brain's infrastructure? This Sense Of Self (S.O.S.) is only powerfully present so long as the brain is active or healthy. When the subjective S.O.S. is bright and crisp it can inhibit the brain's habitual automatic mode of operating. I like to refer to this S.O.S. as a call for help when the brain needs to be monitored or changed. This S.O.S., or call for help, cannot be observed as an enduring agent, but yet causes activity in the brain when it is active in the present moment. When the brain is hijacked, the S.O.S. seems powerless.

I had witnessed such a hijacking by a young prisoner who was paged to the Chaplain's office because of an emergency at home. I had watched broadside changes processed differently nearly every day. This one really caught my attention. His name was Chris and as he walked in Fr. Dinger's office he knew something terrible had happened.

"What's up?"

"Your family wants you to call home,

immediately."

"What happened?"

"Sit down, Son, and I'll dial the number for you."

After dialing the number, Fr. handed Chris the receiver.

"Hi, Mom. What's up?"

Chris, released his grip on the receiver as if he was shot. He slid off his chair to the floor at Fr.'s feet. He cried out in agony,

"NO! NO! It can't be true. NO!"

He then curled up in a prenatal position, crying helplessly on the floor. As I watched through Fr. Dinger's office windows an inmate appeared beside me and asked,

"What's happening in there? That's my homeboy and co-defendant."

"I don't know for sure. He just called home and is clearly devastated."

I followed as his co-defendant rushed into Fr.'s office. Chris looked up at his homeboy and said,

"Those fuckers said they would protect my family if I testified against gang members. Those motherfuckers didn't do a fucking thing to protect my family."

"Chris, it will be okay."

"It will be okay? How can it be okay?

They shot and killed my sister!"

Chris stood up and began grabbing stacks of books off the shelf in Fr. Dinger's office and screamed,

"How the fuck is it going to be okay? They killed my sister! They're going to kill my whole fucking family and I can't do a fucking thing about it!"

His words chilled my blood.

Chris' co-defendant tackled him and pushed him into a chair and grabbed the arm rests. He verbally begged God to intervene as he held Chris in the chair with all his might. Now in a frenzied rage, Chris broke free from his co-defendant's grip and was tipping over chairs as Fr. picked up the phone to dial the deuces.

"Father, please don't dial the deuces," I pleaded.

"He'll be okay."

Chris stopped and looked at us and screamed,

"They killed my sister and my mother is next!"

Fr. Dinger stood frozen, holding the phone as if a statue.

Everything seemed to slow down as Chris lashed out again. His eyes were glowing with rage as his homeboy tackled Chris again. This time he held Chris down in another chair with his shoulder buried into Chris' chest. Chris could hardly get his breath and started to collapse before he began tapping his co-defendant's back, shouting,

"They killed my sister because I testified, next is my mother and then they will kill me when I am released. There's nothing I can do to stop them."

Chris at last ceased struggling and collapsed.

"Thank you, Jesus," his co-defendant whispered.

They both were crying as Fr. Dinger picked up the phone and made a call. Moments later the medics came and gave Chris a shot. Chris' behavior then instantly changed from violence to passiveness.

"What did they give him?" I asked.

"Just something to keep him peaceful," Fr. hinted.

"But Father, what did they give him? Why are they treating him with drugs rather than offering him love and support? Why, Father, why?"

Fr. left his office without answering.

BRAIN CHANGE

The medics rolled Chris off in a wheelchair, completely disconnected from his prior rage. It reminded me of my accident.

I reflected to myself how God has failed as an interventionist. Drugs are now the tool to make it all feel better. Drugs saturate our brains and override our Sense Of Self, our anger, rage, and hatred. No wonder everyone is using drugs and alcohol as tools for comfort. As with Chris, God did not intervene in this craziness and again drugs were the tool used to change his reality. As I was standing in Fr.'s office in shock, Chris' homeboy came up to me and whispered,

"Chris is in a war he cannot win, nor can it be stopped. It will have to run its course, probably for a couple of generations now."

I looked at him and saw the tears running down his cheeks, then he hunched his shoulders in helplessness and walked off. I thought,

"How can we let this run its course through generations of kids?"

I saw Chris a few times on the compound with his eyes glazed over, walking as if in slow motion. We inmates called that walk the Thorazine Shuffle.

The efficiency of drugs and an

interventionist understanding of God must be the reason why so many inmates like Chris get mentally hijacked and why prison staff use drugs to maintain some sort of order. When we trust an interventionist God, it puts our Sense Of Self to sleep. This is a crisis. And the problem intensifies when the inmates are released and suddenly taken off their medication. Because their brains are habituated to drugs as a tool for nonviolence, they are released back into society with a brain unequipped to function civilly.

* * *

Prior to prison, I had acquired degrees in philosophy and sociology from the University of Wisconsin-Platteville campus. When I witnessed Chris' behavior I reflected on my past exposure to Descartes' philosophical question or premise as to what is real. As Descartes' doubted each thing appearing real he came to the final belief he couldn't doubt the existence of the doubter. The doubter had to be real to doubt the existence of everything else. Even doubting its own existence proved it existed by the act of doubting. Many people know Descartes for his famous words,

"*Cogito ergo sum.*"

"I think, therefore I am."

The book *Descartes' Error* by Dr. António Damásio, a neurologist, intrigued me by claiming that Descartes had errored. Dr. Damásio didn't find a doubter during his research on the brain. Descartes believed there was a body and an imprisoned thinker or what was known as the homunculus, a little person, or the doubter; I will add the Self. Neurologists didn't find an agent or Self in the brain processing incoming data and making a choice or decision. Dr. Damásio's research showed a very complex mutual connection between the body and the brain. The thinker, doubter, homunculus or Self wasn't found as an enduring agent that would live independent of the body but rather a S.O.S. common in the midst of the neurological landscape of each brain. It is common to each of us and dependent on the life and health of the brain.

To think of each Sense Of Self as the same and not individually different in each brain was challenging for me. I was raised in a Protestant belief system where God was an interventionist and I was an individual imprisoned in my body and would live on after the death of my body. Neurological research was challenging my basic belief system and at the same time supporting my growing belief that my accident contributed to my lack of compassion and criminal behavior. A person without the presence of a S.O.S. is a dangerous individual in any community – even the prison community. It was becoming neurologically possible that my life lacked compassion and a powerful Sense Of Self because my brain's landscape was rattled and changed as a result of my accident. This perspective was exciting and at the same time frightening. What if my willingness for criminal thinking emerged as a result of my accident, and what if criminal thinking emerges as a result of our brain's landscape development? If this is true, who is responsible for the development or damage of our adult citizens and new offspring's brains? An honest and open conversation regarding this perspective will be a slippery slope to say the least, but it is one we must have since neurology is challenging many of our past beliefs. The sooner we start this conversation, the better.

BRAIN CHANGE

* * *

Let us consider gradual brain reconstruction through the power of our daily self-talk. My mother repeated her thoughts every day, reconstructing her neurological positive brain landscape into a neurological negative brain. This repetition of her thoughts clearly reconstructed the landscape of her brain. Her thoughts reconstructed her brain from being the positive hopeful person I knew for years into a bitter and hateful person I could not recognize. If her internal self-talk rehearsals would have given her brain permission to kill this anonymous woman, she would have been held solely responsible for her actions. I would have said,

"That couldn't be. That is not the kind of mother I knew."

Consider another example of the power of such self-talk:

Rodney, my angry or happy cellie. Rodney mentally rehearsed his hatred toward his ex-wife daily for at least three years. I watched its effect on the gradual reconstruction of his brain's landscape. Neurologists tell us we have 60,000 thoughts each day and 95% of them are the same every day. We spend 60% of the time talking to ourselves and 40% of the time talking to others. We're yakking 24/7 about the same thing, over and over. This self-coaching process for Rodney happened when laying on his bunk, clinching his fists, and releasing his grip. One day I asked Rodney if that was an isometric exercise. He smiled and said,

"When I clinch my fists I am rehearsing how I am going to kill my wife."

I was shocked and said we don't need to talk about this anymore. As time went on Rodney would share tidbits about his life with Tina, his wife, and why he was angry with her. Rodney was a cooker, convicted of manufacturing methamphetamine, for a motorcycle club which was and still is a dangerous occupation. When he was busted he left his wife several thousands of dollars in cash and some of his most valued personal belongings. Rodney had been in prison about 40 months when I met him. After I became his cellie, he found out from his brother that his wife had no money left and was in another relationship. Rodney left behind an expensive pair of elephant skin boots, a Stetson cowboy hat, a huge shiny cow horn belt buckle and a yellow Corvette. His stash of money was gone and his boots, hat, and belt buckle were now being worn by his wife's new boyfriend who now also drove Rodney's yellow Corvette. Rodney spent most of his time mentally calculating how he would find his wife and how he'd kill her. He explained how his wife loved fireplaces, and how he'd advertise cords of firewood for a specially low price. He described how he would deliver the wood and when he got in the house, he would kill her and her boyfriend. Rodney coached his brain each day as did Mom. He lifted weights and pounded on the boxing bag for years until he was physically scary to look upon. If he hit you, he would either break your bones or crush your organs. Upon release, Rodney's neurological landscape was a mouse trap, ready to snap. He gave me a hug and said he was going to be living a good life. I asked him to forget about his money, hat, boots, and car. He laughed and said,

"Lyle, that was all just a joke. I really don't care."

His wife, some prison staff, and I knew he would appear out of the blue one day. A few months after his release I received a letter. At first glance I saw it was from a state prison out west. I wish I'd have saved it, but it was lost in the years of moving and cleaning out my accumulated papers. It read that Rodney wanted me to come out west and testify on behalf of his character. He was charged with first degree murder. I panicked thinking I could somehow be caught up in a conspiracy to murder his wife. I called my attorney, Thomas Halloran, who advised me to relax and let it unfold. In a couple of weeks I was called to my case manager's office for a phone call from Rodney's prosecutor. She introduced herself and then asked if I had been Rodney's cellie prior to his release. I confessed. Her next question was straight forward.

"Mr. Wildes, did Rodney ever say he was going to kill anybody when he got out of prison?"

I thought for a moment and said,

"Everyone in here has said at least once they are going to kill somebody when they get out. Who did Rodney kill?"

She continued,

"Did Rodney ever talk about some woman named Mary?"

"Yes."

"Did Rodney ever write to her or talk with her on the phone?"

"No, he never corresponded with her. He used to tell me stories about Mary. He said he had to stay away from her because she always got him in trouble. He described her as a petite, attractive woman. When they went to a bar she would find the biggest guy in there and ask him to help her get away from Rodney. She would claim in her tender way,

'He is holding me against my will.'

She would return and sit down beside Rodney as if nothing happened. After a couple of drinks the big guy would approach Rodney and say,

'This young lady tells me she can't get away from you. Is that true?'

Rodney would laugh and turn to Mary, telling her to straighten out her shit. Rodney was soon in a fight, brutally beating up the big guy before leaving the bar. On the way out Rodney would tell Mary,

'You have to stop doing that crazy shit.' Mary would laugh and jump in his truck. Just listening to him tell all his stories I felt he really liked Mary, but he was going to have to stay away from her upon his release."

"Mr. Wildes, Rodney killed Mary."

"How? Why would he kill Mary?"

"Well, we do know 'how.' Rodney tells us that he, Mary, and another man who we haven't yet found were talking and Rodney got angry and hit Mary with his fist driving her chin bone up into her brain. Then he took her body and secretly buried it in his friend's backyard.

"Oh God! What's going to happen now?"

"After talking with you, I do not see a motive. Rather, something happened that triggered Rodney. I suppose Rodney was angry when he was released and he took it out on the first person who triggered him. Mr. Wildes, thank you for your time and comments. You have helped me understand that Rodney had no intentions of killing Mary. She certainly was not his target."

"No, Mary wasn't his target."

I hung up the phone and couldn't let go of Rodney's situation. It has troubled me for years and I still believe that an innocent woman died because Rodney spent years repeating the self-talk, reconstructing his brain's neurological landscape into a killer. Mary just happened to be in the wrong place at the wrong time. Rodney killed a woman he really liked. His neurological landscape was in a place to kill, we know from hindsight. Rodney is the most extreme example of the power of self-talk coaching the reconstruction of a brain in a prison cell without anyone intervening. Some nights I lie in my bed, angry at myself because a good man killed an innocent woman. I often feel I didn't do enough, knowing that Rodney was developing the neurological landscape of a killer on autopilot. Rodney had to take full responsibility for the crime because the law could not see the makings of a killer as I had witnessed during our incarceration together.

I hold firmly to the belief there are thousands of men and many women coming out of the prison environment after years of living where violence is legitimized by the prison culture. There will be men, children, and women who will hurt or kill or be hurt or killed as a byproduct of negative self-talk during years of incarceration. At this time, no one will step up and take responsibility nor will the law hold anyone responsible for these violent crimes except for the prisoner. Those who developed the man-made prison environment where the brain's landscape is transformed through negative self-talk

BRAIN CHANGE

rehearsals hour after hour, day after day, month after month, year after year take no responsibility for the brain's reconstruction and the resulting negative behavior. Many still reject the creeping, transforming power of the negative self-talk taking place in our tax-supported prison environments. Who will step up and take responsibility for rejecting the power of the brain's negative self-talk in a prison environment?

* * *

Fr. Dinger had been my boss for more than six years when our journey suddenly came to an end. Fr. Dinger kept saying he was going to retire, but he never told any of us the date. One day, Fr. didn't come to work and we were simply told that Fr. retired. Shortly after Fr. Dinger retired, my experiences at Milan also came to an end. They were moving a number of prisoners from Milan to open a new prison in Elkton, OH, and I was one of them. While facilitating the PMA class at Milan, the focus of the class was on our thinking, beliefs, actions and consequences. At that time, I was learning more about the brain and started to feel a need to change the content of the class. I had come to believe that happiness and one's meaning in life were no longer simply connected to our thinking, beliefs, actions, and consequences. After leaving Milan in 1997, I realized I had been stuck in a certain way of thinking about change and how to facilitate it. Being transferred to the new facility at Elkton was an opportunity to change the name of the PMA class and its content. I wanted to base the class on neurology and less on our techniques, tools, and anger management skills. My new sponsor was Dr. Caroline Frazer and she sponsored the implementation of my new class now known as the Positive Attitude Development (PAD) class. I chose the name 'Positive Attitude Development' because in my experience I believe that change is a process of reconstructing our neurological landscape and deconstructing our old neurological pathways, learned values, and beliefs. Dr. Frazer introduced me to a book entitled *To Forgive Is Human* by Michael E. McCullough, Steven J. Sandage, and Everett L. Worthington Jr. It was in this book that I was exposed to the importance of forgiveness:

"Unforgiven hurts are like rocks tossed into a peaceful sea, creating ripples and turbulence that disturb the placid surface. If many hurts occur at nearly the same time, the previously calm water of our lives is churned into white caps of distress. Recall a time you have been hurt. If you bitterly held onto the hurt, it disturbed your peace. Forgiveness is a place of calm in an angry sea. Forgiveness is often sought but less often found."

At Milan there was a sea of anger, fear, and violence. Talking about managing one's anger or fear seemed ridiculous, and finding a way to let go and reconstruct the brain's landscape was my new focus. I started to understand anger and fear were based on certain values and beliefs which manifested in our negative attitude. Mom bitterly held onto the hurt because of her values and beliefs regarding what is unforgivable, which created her sea of anger. To imagine the smoke carrying those violations out of sight as she maintained her values and beliefs supporting her anger was difficult for me to

BRAIN CHANGE

defend. If she couldn't let go, what makes change possible? And then, what process could make letting go or change possible for Mom and the men in my class? It was becoming more evident to me that letting go meant deconstructing one's learned values and supporting belief systems, then reconstructing one's values and beliefs based on the kind of a person you want to BE rather the kind of person you became. At Elkton I reflected back on my thinking as a chapel clerk. From my position in the chapel clerk's chair, prisoners were asked to turn their problems over to God or Jesus and relax. Now, the PAD class taught that chaos and recidivism were connected to our learned values and belief systems which supported our criminal lifestyle.

The new PAD class participants rolled up their sleeves and identified their Core Values necessary for being the kind of person they wanted to BE, even in prison. Looking back at the chapel clerk's chair gave me a clear understanding of the importance of one's Core Values and one's supporting beliefs. When putting thousands of prisoners in small locked areas where compassion is not valued and violence

BRAIN CHANGE

and hatred are a way of life, chaos is the inevitable result on any prison compound. There it was, standing right in front of me. If you value violence, you will use it. If you value compassion and empathy, you will treat everyone kindly. Milan was a culture of anger, hatred, and violence. In my life, I was developing the values of compassion and kindness and I began to experience a quality life, even in prison. I was shocked to see the different effects occurring with different values and beliefs. Many of the prisoners at Elkton were illegal immigrants, a class of people in prison and not having an out date, but rather an unknown deportation date. Elkton's community of anger was a justice issue.

* * *

If we want to understand ways to de-criminalize men and women in our prisons we must see the power and importance of Self-talk, Core Values, and their supporting Beliefs. Core Values are powerful for an institution, an agency, a corporation, or an individual. When you have lived in a prison culture as long as I have, believing

BRAIN CHANGE

individuals are responsible for a crime does not match my experience. My personal research and experiences with the brains of prisoners contradict present-day beliefs about criminal behavior. When we see different profiles in the brain's landscapes we also see different behaviors. The brain is the organ of all behaviors, and there is no decision-making agent found within the brain's network. It is a systemic network and functions in accordance with the profile at the time of a stimuli. It is time to see the difference between an enduring agent, i.e. homunculus or Self being responsible as a decision-maker and a developed network responding to stimuli in accordance to the condition of that landscape. We know things now about the brain which were unavailable to the early philosophers and logicians who used self-reflection to understand their own existence. Self-reflection has given birth to the belief of the existence of a doubter or a Self as a thinker and decision maker with freewill. This is in contradiction to some neurologists who haven't been able to locate a specific brain area or homunculus that gathers data and makes correct decisions out of freewill. It is my belief that we need to let go of the idea of a Self as a decision-maker with freewill, one that is corrupted prior to birth and is susceptible to the temptations of worldly pleasures, struggling to be vindicated by some distant creator before its release from its prison, the body. We need to challenge the belief of a Self born out of self-reflection, releasing ourselves of its limitations and chains. The release of this mistaken belief will have a Copernican effect on the way we treat crime, heroism, and each other. We must replace it with the development, health, and importance of our brain and this planet. When we release the birth of a Self through self-reflection and replace it with a suspended subjective Sense Of Self evolving out of the condition of our brain's neural network, we will understand love, hatred, prejudice, and crime differently and more accurately. Our brains and its suspended Sense Of Self have evolved out of the soup of this earth and the experience of its evolution. I believe we will find the Sense Of Self with a texture of altruism within its midst, out of sight of the eye of science. We need to discover new words and metaphors to understand and explain our suspended Sense Of Self. I will say more about this later.

BRAIN CHANGE

* * *

The power of Self-talk, Sense Of Self, a call for help, and reframing our experiences came to light while facilitating the PAD class at Elkton. As part of the final class I asked the participants to share what they were taking with them after completing the PAD class. One young man's perspective about being in the present moment and using the power of the S.O.S. to reframe a difficult situation brought it all together for me. This young, special black man shuffled in his chair before procceding up front to tell what he was taking from the class. He began with a powerful, demanding deep voice,

"At first I was just going to pass and say nothing. But I decided I needed to let Lyle and all of you know what I am benefiting from this class. A few weeks ago I decided to call home while waiting for the compound to open up for the ten-minute movement so I could come to our weekly PAD class. When I called home, my family was worried, upset, and angry because I hadn't returned their phone call. Come to find out, my dad died unexpectedly a few weeks earlier and was buried without me knowing about his death or being able to be with my family. My family notified the Chaplain but apparently he didn't write it down and forgot to tell me. When I heard they had called the Chaplain and he never told me, I was instantly enraged, or as Lyle would call it, mentally hijacked. I wanted to kill the motherfucker."

Standing before the class, the man's eyes filled with tears and his voice was filled with sadness. He continued,

"When the ten-minute movement was announced I felt that if I ever needed to go to Lyle's class, it's now. So I pulled up my S.O.S. and coached my brain to let it go for now."

He stopped for a moment to gather his thoughts, then continued,

"The Chaplain is one door down in the other direction from our classroom. I'm not sure why, but I came to class and didn't go fuck with the Chaplain. I sat back where I usually sit, only that day I was trembling with anger. Lyle was talking about living in the present moment, the power of our Self-talk, the importance of our Core Values, Beliefs, unforgivable violations and reframing situations. During class, I realized

BRAIN CHANGE

I was dangerously out of control and truly mentally hijacked. I sat back in this very room and listened to Lyle talk about anger being a justice issue. It's not right, it isn't fair, or they should or shouldn't have done that. Lyle said,

'If you reframe your perspective of any situation that is causing you to be angry, your anger will go away.'

I sat here trying to reframe my perspective. I started to believe the Chaplain probably didn't do it on purpose. When he finds out what he did he will certainly feel badly about it and sincerely apologize. I want to tell you here today, I do not condone what the Chaplain did and I still think he's incompetent, but I'm not going to let his negligence affect my behavior. This class is constantly talking about the power of our Self-talk values, beliefs, forgiveness, reframing, and letting go probably saved our incompetent Chaplain's life."

Silence filled the room as this young man paused. Everyone there had experienced some degree of injustice, causing hatred to hijack them, too. When he turned and faced me he said,

"Thank you, Lyle, for teaching this

class. Every week your class has helped me, and I am sure all of us, to monitor our Self-talk, be present in our NOW Box, forgive others, and identify our Core Values and Beliefs. This class has given me an edge of three seconds, which was just long enough to be present in a different way and reframe the situation and let go of my anger. Had I not lived in my three seconds I would be in prison for life because I would have killed the Chaplain one door down the hall. It was that close, guys. Believing the Chaplain did it intentionally would have allowed me to be violent and that belief would have put me in prison for life. The belief he will feel badly and probably ask for forgiveness simply allows me to forgive him and one day go home to my family. I want to thank you, and I am sure my family will, too, when they know what you have done for all of us."

As he walked back to his chair, the room was silent and everyone was humbled by this young man's story. I felt fortunate to have had this young man present, as a gift from the mystery of life, live in his three seconds and apply the PAD process. Doing so had saved him from a life of incarceration. There was no need for another word to be spoken and, as if planned, the building speaker broke the silence.

"The compound is now open for a ten-minute movement."

As everyone silently left the room I understood forgiveness is a process and a gift we give ourselves. It doesn't mean we condone the behavior of others; it means we can reframe the situation and remain safe. My own brain was developing the landscape for a new life of peace and a sense of purpose. I was feeling less mentally starved and more mentally fulfilled. Facilitating my PAD class was fertile soil to blossom wherever planted – yes, even in prison. It's strange how this happens.

* * *

In 1999, a new BOP policy came into affect allowing prisoners with ten years or less remaining in their sentence to be transferred to a camp. I was transferred from Elkton, OH, to the Duluth, MN, prison camp where I encountered a completely different type of prison population. Milan had long-term prisoners, Elkton had a population of deportation prisoners, and Duluth had a population of short timers including a few at the end of several years of incarceration. I was fortunate to immediately implement my PAD class at Duluth. Cindy Helmer became my PAD class supervisor. The Duluth camp setting stimulated me to reflect on my 20 years growing up, 20 years messed up, 20 years locked up, and the teachings of my PAD class. At Duluth I encountered prisoners who had recently lived in the public where I would soon be released. The first major difference I experienced at the Duluth camp was an open compound. We could move around on the compound as soon as the kitchen called for the units to be released for breakfast at 6:00 am. Early one morning on my way to the chow hall, I noticed a paper dancing in the wind headed my way. At times it was whirling as if being carried by intentions. It moved in my direction and slowly tumbled onto the sidewalk in front of me. I quickly stepped on it and reached down and picked it up. It was a brochure advertising Mihaly Csikszentmihalyi, the author of the book *Flow*, who was going to be speaking at the University of Minnesota main campus. I just finished reading his book and thought I would write to the sponsor, Ruth Stricker. I asked if the author could come to the prison compound to be the PAD class graduation guest speaker. Ruth took the time to write back to say he would not be available to come to the prison but then asked about my PAD class. When I found out she owned the award-winning Marsh, a wellness center and spa, I decided to ask if she would be my class graduation guest speaker. She agreed and we started a relationship I enjoy still to this day. Ruth gave an inspiring presentation. She told us,

"Life is not a long marathon you win or lose. Life offers an opportunity for new starts and you don't ever need to think of life as winning or losing."

When Ruth finished, the audience erupted with cheers and a standing ovation. Ruth was talked about on the compound for months afterward. A couple of years later and prior to my being transferred to another federal facility in Yankton, SD, Ruth agreed to come back as the final PAD graduation guest speaker at Duluth. By this time nearly half of the prison compound had participated in PAD classes. Ruth stepped up in front of a filled theater with no standing room remaining. She gave another wonderful message and then ended by asking us to do some t'ai chi. She directed hundreds of men in the theater to hold their arms up in the air and freely sway back and forth. It was such a wonderful and touching experience to see men filling the theater with movements of peace and compassion. Smiles of joy filled the theater as the men swayed back and forth and Ruth danced so gracefully and eloquently to her special music. When she finished she received a long standing ovation. It was awesome to see how Ruth had moved men who were stressed, anxious, and doubtful to a place of peace, compassion, and hope.

* * *

I was transferred to the Yankton, SD, federal prison camp where I attended the Residential Drug Abuse Program (RDAP) to get a few months taken off my sentence. The Yankton Education Department immediately sponsored my PAD program at their facility. I attended the RDAP full-time and facilitated my PAD class once a week. The RDAP program emphasized rational thinking to show how your feelings and actions are a result of your beliefs, thoughts, and attitude. We discussed the choices we had before us and the choices we made. My PAD class dovetailed nicely with the RDAP program by supporting this belief: we will always make the same decision unless we change our Core Values and their supporting Beliefs. We can act in conflict with our Core Values and supporting Beliefs for a short time, but eventually we will default to the neurological landscape associated with our original learned Core Values and Beliefs. Upon completing the RDAP program I was moved from Yankton, SD, to the Bethel Halfway House in Duluth, MN. At Bethel I was feeling In-Between my prison lifestyle and my new post incarceration lifestyle.

But I never gave up!

"Because change is a process, not an event, that is accomplished by coaching one's brain and accepting help from others."

- Lyle Wildes

Back in 1999, when I was at the Duluth prison camp, I had the good fortune of meeting Brooks Anderson. He was given a 90 day federal sentence for a misdemeanor: unlawful trespassing on a military base at Fort Benning in Columbus, Georgia. A staff member suggested I get to know Brooks. One day while we were both in the prison library I introduced myself to Brooks. We quickly connected and spent time talking about what it was like being in prison for so many years and why I never gave up. After he got to know more about my PAD class, he thought I would be a good addition to the organization in Duluth known as Domestic Abuse Intervention Programs

(DAIP) where Brooks was a board member. Brooks suggested I move to Duluth, MN, and work for DAIP. I appreciated his offer but I would first have to get my supervised release transferred from Wisconsin to the MN U.S. District Courts. Transferring one's release address from one District to another is not easy. Upon Brooks' release and while I was finishing up the last few months of my sentence, he started the process to get my release address changed to Duluth. He talked with his probation officer, Matt Whiting, who gave some resistance at first but granted my transfer to Duluth, MN. While I was still at the Duluth camp Brooks brought a friend, John Clark Pegg, with him to meet me. Brooks and John came back to visit again but this time Brooks brought his partner, Coral McDonnell, and John brought his partner, Lyn Clark Pegg. After our visit John and Lyn offered me a room in their home for the first few months after my release. John and Lyn didn't know me and yet they opened their home to me for three months rent free. As my three months were coming to a close, John and Lyn extended their offer for as long as I needed to get on my feet. I was no longer facilitating my PAD class weekly, and instead

BRAIN CHANGE

had to focus on my reentry. I was surprised my reentry took longer than a few months, but rather a few years. There were times I would catch myself feeling overwhelmed or mentally hijacked, causing me to block out some positive options available to me. I remembered reentry is a process and not an event, as I had taught for years facilitating my PAD class. It was difficult to stay open to the suggestions of my support network.

One day Frank Jewell, Director for Men As Peacemakers and friend of John and Brooks, appeared as if out of the mystery of life. John, Brooks, and I were talking when Frank interrupted and asked,

"Why is everyone so serious?"

Brooks said,

"Lyle just got out of prison and our original employment plans have fallen through. We're not sure where to turn now for a job."

Frank thought for a few minutes, then offered,

"I can give you a job with Men As Peacemakers, but I can only pay $6 per hour."

There was a moment of silence as Frank and everyone waited for my response. I smiled and said,

"Frank, that's a $5.71 per hour raise. I'll take it."

That offer started my post incarceration lifestyle. I was the handyman around Men As Peacemakers for about six months when Frank offered me a position and a raise. My new position involved developing a reentry program for state and federal prisoners coming out of prison. This gave me more exposure to a number of organizations in Duluth and the surrounding areas. This opportunity allowed me to acclimate, accommodate, and assimilate my feeling of being In-Between my prison lifestyle and society. Within a few weeks I was having group meetings at Men As Peacemakers for those coming out of prison. The first few meetings centered on an awareness that reentry is a process and not an event. Developing my own new post incarceration lifestyle was more difficult than I expected. My Self-talk during my incarceration created the belief I could easily find a job, an apartment, a vehicle, and spending money. I quickly realized how distorted my thinking was about letting go of my prison lifestyle and learning to embrace my post-incarceration lifestyle. This process clearly determined the quality of my life. I was facilitating my reentry program and dealing with my own reentry problems at the same time. I found myself feeling In-Between my life of incarceration and the life as a citizen. I often experienced myself resisting the suggestions of my support network. I thought I knew more about what I needed than they did. While deeply involved in my reentry process I was invited to share meals with Brooks, Coral, John and Lyn who were sincerely interested in supporting me. It was truly a process of trusting my support network and developing the lifestyle of a respected community citizen. I was now working for $12 per hour and getting overwhelmed trying to find a place to live who accepted someone with a felony, buy a vehicle with no credit, and believe this odd new legal lifestyle is fun. In my PAD class I kept emphasizing the importance of remaining calm and living in the present moment. Now, I was having to apply my teachings in real life. It wasn't as easy as I made it sound in my PAD class. In prison I told the PAD participants the present moment is not a day or, as the philosopher Karl Popper wrote,

BRAIN CHANGE

it being only one second long, but rather seven seconds long. I described the present moment as being three seconds long. The present moment is between the two seconds emerging and becoming your present moment, and the two seconds fading out and becoming your past. I also like to use the metaphor of a water fountain bubbling straight up out of the ground and breaking off, leaving a constant bubble of changing steady water at the top. At the bubbling point the water is neither coming up to form the bubble or falling away from the bubble. The constant changing yet steady bubbling represents the present moment where I experienced my incarceration. The record will show I was incarcerated for 585,792,410 seconds but I only experienced prison life as In-Between the emerging and fading two seconds or the emerging and falling water. My experience of incarceration happened in the changing, yet steady, present moment of three seconds. It has nothing to do with time but rather with an eternal changing yet steady present moment. My past is the fading two seconds or the falling water and my future is the emerging two seconds or the approaching water. Living In-Between the emerging and fading two seconds or the rising and falling water is all there is. Being in the present moment is living between the not-yet and the has-been separated by a span of three seconds. When I realized the S.O.S. could determine the quality of those precious three seconds, it made them even more precious and mysterious. I, as the S.O.S., was free to live a quality life within the limits of incarceration and not forced to live a life determined by my incarceration. Everyone determines the texture or quality of their present moment regardless of circumstances. Being able to determine the quality of our three seconds allows us to be as happy as we can ever be.

* * *

Because each of us were experiencing peaks and valleys in our reentry process I shared Coach Jim Tressel's peaks and valleys story. Years prior to my release Coach Jim Tressel, at that time the Head Football Coach at Youngstown State University, came to the Elkton facility as the PAD graduation guest speaker. He gave an inspiring message for all of us. Coach told us how Youngstown's

BRAIN CHANGE

football team had never won a conference championship but it was Coach Tressel's belief this team was capable of being next year's conference champions. The Youngstown athletic staff never displayed the yearly football championship flags on their gymnasium's wall. Coach Tressel requested they be mounted immediately. After the flags of past champions were mounted, Coach asked his football team to look up at the mounted flags and tell him which school's flag would be represented as this year's champions. The football players named some of the other colleges, but Coach Tressel corrected them.

"Guys, it is going to be us!"

A shocked group of young men questioned Coach Tressel's claim. However, after trusting their coaches' abilities, those young men won that year's championship and their college flag was on their gym wall. Coach again in 1993, 1994, and 1997. As Coach Tressel was telling his victory story, I realized Coach had to trust his process if they were ever going to win a championship. In telling his story he said,

"I would like to talk about the peaks and valleys players experience in becoming great football players. Every great football players face difficult times in their football career – first an upturn, then a downturn followed by another upturn. During the downturns some players give up while others see the difficulty as temporary and an opportunity to become better."

Coach Tressel's drawing on the white board looked like a stock market's chart with dips and spikes, but at the end of the day it was at its highest point. Coach continued,

"When the great running backs experience a valley, some give up while others watch videos of the defense and learn ways to get around them. This allows them to become a stronger running back than before. This process of enjoying the peaks and learning in the valleys is necessary to become the best running back or defensive player during their college career. What I want to stress is, the thinking the players came into college with was not sufficient to get them to their next level of playing. It is important to embrace the valleys and reframe them as an opportunity to become the best they can be. When players are performing well they seldom reach a new level. In fact, many of us can become complacent. Many of you here today are in your valley. Embrace it by watching the tapes of your life, pay attention to your errors, let go of your mistakes, and live in the present moment. Monitor your Self-talk and mentally practice what you need to do to get yourself to the next level of success you desire."

Coach closed by saying,

"Remember to learn in the valleys of your life. Embrace them for they are the fertile soil for your personal growth."

As the men were giving Coach Tressel a standing ovation, I realized Fr. Dinger's comments to me about fertile soil was the same message from Coach Tressel. Fertile soil is everywhere if we are willing to reframe the valley or situation as Coach Tressel suggested.

* * *

I found it important to share with the participants the dangers of getting mentally hijacked during a valley. Getting caught in a thunderstorm of rage and anger is always a justice issue. It's not fair. They should or shouldn't have done something. The following story is a radical example of being on automatic pilot and not living in our present moment during one of our thunderstorms of emotion. There was this young man who came to the chapel clerk's office door and rested his elbows on the semi-stable half door counter. He looked exhausted as many men do when they come to see a Chaplain. Without looking up, the young man asked,

"Is there a Chaplain I can talk to? I need to talk to somebody."

I recognized the sound of exhaustion, desperation, and hopelessness in his voice.

"Yes sir, I'll take you to one right now."

I introduced the sad young man to the Chaplain on duty.

"Chaplain, this young man needs to talk with you."

"Come in. Sit down. Tell me what's going on."

The young man wasted no time.

"My wife just came to visit me and she's not going to bring our two boys back to visit me anymore. She's going to divorce me. She's really angry at me. I don't know what to do."

The Chaplain reached over and took the young man's hands.

"What's your name?"

"Ron."

"Okay, Ron. Let's pray about this."

The Chaplain closed his eyes and began to pray as Ron looked confused. I am sure Ron wasn't a Christian as he looked up at me as if asking,

"What the fuck is this about?"

The Chaplain continued to pray,

"Our Heavenly Father, we come before you today because of our brother, Ron."

He finally ended his prayer "in the name of our Lord and our Savior, Jesus Christ. Amen."

The Chaplain opened his eyes and released the young man's wet and trembling hands. He looked even more exhausted, defeated, and angrier than before he came to the chapel.

"Okay, Ron. Let's trust in God to work in our hearts."

I pulled the defeated Ron up out of his chair. He began shuffling aimlessly down the hallway as if nowhere to go. He was defeated and exhausted and lost his ability to care anymore. Ron was clearly mentally hijacked.

When we were out of the range of the

BRAIN CHANGE

Chaplain, I called out:

"Ron, can we talk for a minute? I've been in prison a few years and have felt the way you're feeling right now . . . please?"

Out of his mouth came a weak whisper,

"No. There's nothing to talk about anymore."

Ron shuffled down the hallway toward the exit door. I followed him, afraid of what might happen next. He suddenly turned into the bathroom and locked himself in the first of three stalls. I quietly moved into the stall next to Ron and listened. Because he was mentally hijacked, he didn't know I was in the stall next to him. It's amazing how narrow-minded we become when we get hopelessly hijacked. Gut-wrenching sobs filled the quiet empty bathroom. His tears were dripping on the cold concrete floor in front of his shoes. I pictured him crying with his elbows on his knees and his hands over his face. I sat in that stall a number of times just like that myself. Sitting on the commode roughly eighteen inches from him, I wondered what I could do to relieve some of his pain. The silence was overwhelming as I thought,

"How can God remain silent in such an intense and profound moment of sadness?

Doesn't God care about this man? Is there even a God?"

As I refocused, I noticed the backs of Ron's shoes were broken down. His sobs still ring in my ears yet today. There was a break in his sobbing leaving a screaming silence of anticipation. The silence was broken as his blood splattered on the floor and his feet started to dance. His blood crept outward as his shoes were splashing in the growing pool of blood and then again, another gush hit the cold concrete. I bolted out of the stall and into the main corridor whistling for an officer. The guard dialed the deuces, calling for backup as he rushed into the bathroom. The sound of jingling keys and the thumping of guards boots filled the complex. An officer yelled at me,

"Get back to work, inmate!"

I knew they didn't want inmates watching these kinds of messes nor did I really want to experience it myself, so I headed back to the chapel clerk's chair.

As the Chaplain was running toward the bathroom, I yelled at him,

"So, let's put it in God's hands, huh? Your God remained silent and let another dad kill himself. He had to use violence to

BRAIN CHANGE

find peace."

The Chaplain looked stunned as a Lieutenant yelled at me,

"Get your ass back to your designated area and shut the fuck up, inmate, or you're going to the hole!"

I sat in the Chapel clerk's chair with my elbows on my knees and my hands over my ears crying because I didn't stop him. I was sitting only eighteen inches from this young man, and I didn't have a way to stop him from using violence to find some peace. Damn it, we kill each other in prison and now we're killing ourselves. Prison is causing us to prepare for our death and not for our lives yet to be lived. There is an extremely thin membrane between feeling connected and feeling hopeless, between being hijacked and finding calmness and when it rips, it's over. I could have leaped over the thin partition and saved his life, but I didn't.

"Why didn't I? Why didn't I? Why?"

I later heard that Ron had slashed both of his arms. Ron had been sentenced to 15 years for a drug case and was told by his wife during their visit that the Court of Appeals affirmed his conviction. For Ron's wife, the Court of Appeals was the final word meaning Ron was a liar and an evil drug dealer, which was a deal breaker for her. Did God hear the Chaplain's prayer for help and still allow Ron to kill himself, leaving two boys without a dad? The brain's landscape of chemicals, electrical activities, and pathways are connected to the damage done by the prison environment and must be addressed differently. I saw daily the massive power of prisoners coaching their brains. Coaching a brain makes a difference, but to ask God to intervene gives false hope and frees the prisoner and the Chaplain of taking any responsibility for future action.

* * *

It is important to understand the brain after it passes through the birth canal with an infrastructure ready to be developed for its survival. Its original infrastructure of interacting neural pathways, synapses, and chemistry supports the body's heartbeat and ability to digest, eliminate, and maintain a respiratory rhythm. With this in place, the remaining infrastructure is gradually changed or purged to create a neurological network that will function as an individualized systemic process. Each brain's individualized process contains its own unique habitual responses or no response to its situational experience, internal or external. This systemic process eventually develops and runs on automatic pilot. There is no central location or homunculus located in the brain knowing right from wrong that processes incoming data.

* * *

Within this systemic process is a plasticity giving the brain the ability to change itself. Change can broadside the brain as with my accident, or change can be initiated from within the brain as I practiced during my incarceration. Both of these forms of change require the brain to let go of the way life used to be and adjust to the way life is going to be now or in the near future. Since the brain has plasticity it is considered strong enough to resist change, yet weak enough to be changed if coached correctly. Knowing change is a constant in everyday life, it is important to understand a moment in time when the brain is In-Between two lifestyles. All change – except broadsided sudden change – causes the brain to feel In-Between for a period of time, but if the brain gets caught in the stage of change for too long it can become pathological. The stages of In-Between are: encountering the change; processing the change; and the new lifestyle of change. Labeling this moment between the old lifestyle and the new one as In-Between implies the brain feels awkward, frustrated, and confused until it adjusts to or integrates the change into its neural network. This In-Between is the span of time needed for the brain to morph or develop new pathways and purge the old neural pathways, synapses, and resulting chemistry. This time called In-Between is necessary to coach the brain to let go of its resistance and embrace the development of a neurological network that supports a new lifestyle.

The present perspective on changing behavior is based on cognitive skill-building methods for managing your symptoms. This method does not consider the brain's hardwired neurological network holding the old behavior in place. Recent neurological research shows how the old neurological network must be reconstructed through appropriate neural exercises to create change. Ways of reconstructing the brain's old habitual landscape will revolutionize our ways for addressing addictions and violent behaviors. We must draw our attention to the resistance of understanding the importance of the physical brain in the process of change.

Let's go back a moment to understand how each brain's systemic process contains its own unique neurological network to act or react to experiences, internally or externally. Since the brain doesn't know the difference between good or bad, it learns what to do habitually. Then it repeats its behavior and resists any attempts to change it. Within each individualized neural landscape, a Sense Of Self eventually emerges capable of coaching its host. This emerging S.O.S. is the same in each brain. There is no *you* or *me*, but rather a subjective sense of being – our *Sense of Self* – present in each brain. The Sense Of Self had no part in the learning behavioral process, but it does have the power to inhibit any of the brain's learned behaviors.

As I said above, the Sense Of Self is the same in every brain. Picture the brain as a pane of glass in a wall the sun shines through. The light behind the pane of glass is vast and of one essence. The texture of each window

BRAIN CHANGE

glass determines the kind of sunlight on this side of the pane. The brain is a vessel in which pure energy flows. The energy behind the brain is vast and of one essence. The neurological landscape of each brain determines the quality of the individualized behaviors. Today, the role of the Sense Of Self must be as a brain coach rather than being asleep or disinterested in the brain's learned negative habitual behaviors. For many generations there was no need for the Sense Of Self to be interested in monitoring the brain's behavior.

Change didn't happen at the rate we are experiencing it today. Generations ago the brain probably had to deal with broadsided change such as volcanoes, fires, sickness, starvation, earthquakes, or damaging storms. The brain is efficient, making sense out of data and at some point makes the data its values and beliefs that are transferred into its actions. This process creates the neural network supporting its invisible values and beliefs in regard to its internal and external experiences. The brain has never pulled up its values and beliefs and given them names. The brain doesn't openly know its values and beliefs, yet it lives them out during its three seconds. These developed or caught invisible values and beliefs are suspended in the neural network and have become the rudder of an individual's actions. Its invisible core values and beliefs create a cloud among each of us known as our attitude.

Because of the power of our attitude, I called my cognitive behavioral process the Positive Attitude Development (PAD) Process. We must develop an awareness of the importance of our attitude. Each brain's neurological landscape produces its unique attitude. Our attitude determines the look on our faces, the way we sit, walk, talk, and interact. When we encounter someone's attitude, it quickly tells us something important about that individual. Attitudes either welcome us or turn us away. More people are hired and fired because of their attitude than all other reasons put together. You can be hired because you have a needed skill, but you will be let go if you have a bad or negative attitude. I like to think of one's attitude as a cloud hanging around each of us. Out of that cloud rains our daily thoughts.

Deepak Chopra writes in his book *Ageless body, Timeless Mind*:

BRAIN CHANGE

"We have sixty thousand thoughts a day and ninety-five percent of them are the same every day."

Not only do we keep repeating the same thoughts every day, but 80% of those thoughts are negative. With 80% of our thoughts being negative, it is difficult to sit down at the end of the day and say,

"This was a great day."

Instead we say with sarcasm,

"Just another day in paradise."

When something positive happens in our lives we tell one person, but when something negative happens we tell eleven people. If someone says something negative, we tend to follow up with,

"If you think that's bad let me tell you what happened to me."

We are quick to point out something more negative then the story just told. When someone says,

"You won't believe what a wonderful thing happened to me yesterday."

We are not likely to say,

"If you think that was good, let me tell you the good thing that happened to me."

Instead we tend to downplay or reframe

the positive situation, getting them "back to reality." With our attitude raining our thoughts, these repeated thoughts generate our actions. If the brain repeats a thought often enough it is going to act on it. For example, if you hang out with anglers long enough and discuss the art of fishing, you will go fishing. If you hang out in a salon and talk about hairstyles long enough you will end up getting a trim or haircut. If you continue repeating the same thought and generating the same action, your brain will develop that habit. Understanding the power and role of habits has been one of the most important insights from my prison experience. The brain's formed habits were caught from its experiences and then it resists any attempts to change them. Knowing the brain is an habitual organ, it is no surprise that it runs off triggers and buttons. I am sure my reader has had one of their buttons pushed or triggers pulled. When that happens, the brain responds on automatic pilot. Knowing the brain runs on autopilot, we ought not be surprised that change is difficult. With most cognitive programs the brain can change its behavior for a while but it will often default to its

BRAIN CHANGE

neural supported habits. The PAD cognitive behavioral program is based on neurology. Neurology has discovered a plasticity within the brain, allowing it to change itself. Neural plasticity allows the brain to be strong enough to resist change yet weak enough to be changed when properly coached to form a new neural network, creating a wonderful life. This process takes roughly 60 hours of practicing the new habit to change itself. This was the second insight I learned during my incarceration. Plasticity and a Sense Of Self were included in the original infrastructure of the brain. Generations ago the brain had less need for plasticity for addressing daily or moment-by-moment changes. The brain hasn't needed the powerful influence of a Sense Of Self to inhibit the brain's habits it learned during its earlier consistent herd-like environment. Today the brain is driven to change more often and rapidly than ever before. The S.O.S., or a call for help, must be strengthened to coach the brain through this present time of In-Between by letting go of its resistance and embracing the new developing environment. I like using the powerful metaphor of the rainbow to understand our S.O.S. When certain weather conditions are present a crisp bright rainbow appears in the sky. We can't reach up and pull it down as if it is an entity in the sky. It appears separate from everything, but is simply suspended within the infrastructure of the raindrops. We cannot operate on the human brain and remove a Sense Of Self or its values and beliefs as if entities in the brain. The Sense Of Self subjectively appears or feels separate from everything, but it is simply suspended within the infrastructure of the brain cells. Changing weather conditions can compromise or even remove the rainbow. The rainbow reappears unchanged with the return of certain weather conditions. Likewise, when the neurological landscape changes, our Sense Of Self can become compromised and even disappear. Recall the last time you were under anesthesia and how your Sense Of Self disappeared. The Sense Of Self then reappears unchanged with the removal of the anesthesia. Moments after my accident, the damaged neural networks caused my S.O.S. to become compromised and weakened its ability and its interest in my prior goals and dreams before my accident. This understanding of the connection between brain damage

BRAIN CHANGE

and compromising the Sense Of Self will require new ways to think about and treat illegal, violent, antisocial, and instinctual behaviors. The neurological landscape of the brain supports habitual behavior, and to change habitual behavior we need to change the brain's neural network. This is all about exercising the brain for roughly 60 hours to accomplish a specific purpose. If we don't address changing the brain's neural network, the brain will often default back to its original neural network supported behavior. Over the years I have heard people talk about an awakening that changed their lives. The Sense Of Self doesn't only need to be awakened but, more importantly, strengthened. We have to construct the neural habits to fortify a crisp and strong Sense Of Self. When our S.O.S. is strengthened then it can build a healthy relationship with its host, the brain. It is important that the Sense Of Self builds a healthy relationship with its host to coach it. It has been suspended within the infrastructure of the brain cells for generations and is now needed to coach the brain during these rapidly changing times. The PAD cognitive program stresses the importance of strengthening the S.O.S.

BRAIN CHANGE

and building a healthy relationship with its host to change itself. Many of us let our brains run on autopilot and then wonder why conflict or violence keeps happening. The need to strengthen the S.O.S. is more important today than even ten or twenty years ago. To have our Sense Of Self coach our brains it needs to have a stronger presence in monitoring the brain's actions. Individuals who have successfully stopped smoking or using drugs or alcohol often refer to the strength their Sense Of Self needed to overcome the minute-by-minute waves of urges. This is the brain being coached by a very strong Sense Of Self so the brain doesn't win with its past tactics. The Sense Of Self's role isn't just to inhibit the brain's behaviors. Its role is to coach the brain to create a quality of life with a strong sense of well-being. What is this quality of life? How can we understand where the S.O.S. gets its game plans for coaching the brain to develop this quality of life? What will life be like if the brain surrenders to its Sense Of Self's plan? Why should most brains release their learned behavior caught only a few years ago? Have they become antiquated in a new world? As plasticity and a Sense Of Self are suspended

BRAIN CHANGE

in the midst of the brain cells why, then, couldn't the game plan be suspended in the essence of the Sense Of Self? Tree seeds have suspended within the seed the habits for becoming a tree. We know the embryo has the habits invisibly suspended in its DNA for developing a baby, so why couldn't the Sense Of Self have the habits invisibly suspended within its historical insights for a quality of life? The Sense Of Self is not teleologically designed, but rather historically insightful. The PAD process asks the brain to embrace a new neural landscape supporting the values and beliefs enjoyed throughout its evolution. How can the Sense Of Self writing this book know what is suspended within itself? Some neurologists say our childhood brains have a tendency to be altruistic. Imagine a few babies in a room playing when one of the babies has been caused some pain. As a result of pain the baby begins crying. When the other babies acknowledge the crying baby they surround the baby and want to comfort it. No baby turns its back and avoids the crying child. I believe neurologists have discovered the texture of our S.O.S. as kindness. When I think about the characteristics that have been a key factor for our species' survival generations upon generations, kindness and compassion are those values. They are suspended within our blood and brain cells or as some might say in our hearts and heads. With compassion and kindness as the Core Values or texture of our S.O.S. it is important we strengthen our S.O.S. in the present moment. Violence and hatred have always created resistance, anger and more violence. Remember the story about Chris' sister being shot in a drive-by shooting and how it will be generations before that hatred, anger, and revengeful violence is off the planet. I can't help but remember the generations of violence between the Hatfields and McCoys. Kindness and compassion are associated with justice and fairness. Neurologists understand the endorphins generated by helping or giving something you value to another having a longer lasting sense of well being than accepting a gift from someone else. We hold in high regard Gandhi, Jesus, Confucius, Socrates, Martin Luther King, and others because of their commitment to acts of kindness and compassion. We hold in contempt Al Capone, Jesse James, Hitler, Saddam Hussein, and others because of their commitment to acts of violence,

BRAIN CHANGE

selfishness, and greed. The brain is not a thinking machine. It is a learned instinctual and habitually driven organ. It does not know right from wrong, good from bad, but rather it is an efficient habitual organ. Up until these present rapidly changing times, the learned habits and advice of our elders and their elders was sufficient for survival. Today we need to strengthen our Sense Of Self and give it the deference it deserves. The Sense Of Self holds suspended within its essence the game plan for a meaningful life. Without a strong Sense Of Self the brain runs habitually and often produces chaos and sabotages the lives of its victims. When the Sense Of Self is strengthened and creates the neural landscape and habits within the brain supporting kindness and compassion, we can then enjoy a quality life and so will those whose lives we touch. Our daily habits create our character. Our character is whether we are kind, caring, compassionate, and helpful or whether we are violent, selfish, dangerous, and untrustworthy. Out of our character comes our destiny or quality of life. It is true that our destiny or quality of life will never change until we change our attitude. So the question is, how do we change our attitude?

BRAIN CHANGE

I have developed this neural-focused cognitive behavior process for understanding the steps toward a new quality of life. Our . . .

Attitude – rains thoughts

   Thoughts – generate actions

      Actions – create habits

         Habits – build character

            Character – produces our

               Destiny or Quality Of Life.

Our attitude is the reflection of our individual neural landscapes that support our Core Values and their Beliefs. Our Core Values and Beliefs are suspended in our brain's hardwired neurological landscape. Our habitual neurological landscape was developed during the prenatal period and the first few years of our lives. They were developed to habitually respond to our environment as coached by our caregivers. Once our habitual response was neurologically in place, the brain has the power to resist change, even when change is needed. Today there is a greater need to change for our survival and a sense of well-being because everything in our lives is rapidly changing. The brain's habitual resistance needs a strong, crisp Sense Of Self now more than ever. We are confronting more conflicting values, beliefs, cultures, and ways of life than ever before. Our different values and beliefs are colliding daily. I find it interesting that many of our organizations, agencies, and corporations are so focused on identifying their business' own Core Values, Beliefs, and cultures. As individuals, until now we have not had access to nor any interest in a meaningful process for identifying our Core Values, Beliefs, and Attitudes. Industrial Core Values are listed on some business letterheads, displayed on plaques in their offices, revisited annually, and inside booklets so each employee knows them, and in some cases new employees must support them to be hired. It makes a safe place to work when common Core Values are the boss in the corporate rooms and the world. Below is an example of my personal Core Values:

BRAIN CHANGE

Prior to Prison

My Core Values were: Instant Gratification, Power, and Greed.

My Supporting Beliefs were: If I had the best drugs, lots of money, and the most toys, I win.

My Attitude was: I come first and I don't care or trust anyone else.

My Thoughts were: Acquiring new clients and not getting busted.

My Actions were: Finding new clients and new ways to be safe.

My Habits were: Manufacturing and selling drugs.

My Character was: Being selfish, narcissistic, and violent.

My Destiny was: Losing everything, 22 years in prison.

The Quality of My Life was: Hollow, Helpless, and Hopeless.

Prison and Post Prison

My Core Values are: Transparency, Wellness, and Compassion.

My Supporting Beliefs are: Healthy relationships are important and if any relationship is broken I will miss it very much.

My Attitude is: Trusting and being authentically interested in people.

My Thoughts are: Caring, helping, and compassion.

My Actions are: Sharing my story and listening to people's stories.

My Habits are: Helping others feel valued and asking them curious questions.

My Character is: Caring, listening, and unselfishness.

My Destiny is: Trusted and respected by others and enjoying great memories.

My Quality of My Life is: Peaceful, Meaningful, and Qualitative.

BRAIN CHANGE

Strengthening my S.O.S. to coach my brain to create the neural network for supporting and hosting my new Core Values and Beliefs has kept me from defaulting to my old behaviors and returning to the Federal Bureau of Prisons. My brain's reconstructed neural network now produces the behaviors for creating many great memories.

By focusing only on our thinking and beliefs, we have not addressed the source of the negative behavior. Many relapse and default back to their old behaviors that are still supported by their old neural network. We must change the brain's landscape to host the new Core Values and Beliefs to change the quality of our lives.

I encourage you to identify your Core Values and Beliefs, strengthen your Sense Of Self to coach your brain to create the neural network to host your new Core Values and Beliefs, and enjoy the behaviors that will give you the happiness you seek.

> "Enjoy the process and let your chosen Core Values and supporting Beliefs be the powerful rudder of your life."
> - Lyle Wildes

BRAIN CHANGE

* * *

It is so important for the S.O.S. to be present, strong, and interested today in expressing its insights through coaching its host. Some unique neurological landscapes with a strong S.O.S. have coached their brain for creating symphonies joyful to the ear, art beautiful to the eye, science for expanding our understanding, and compassion for noticing the human suffering in our fragile planet's symphony of life. When the S.O.S. is not present, its host runs automatically off its learned instincts important for another time in history.

Travel and technology have caused our planet to shrink while our different learned neurologically supported mythologies collide as evidenced by daily violence. The time has come for the S.O.S. to coach the brain to let go of its neurologically supported mythologies and create a new common global understanding of our evolving human situation. We have much more in common than differences. We are all connected to our planet in similar ways and we ought to be thinking about our planet as a common cathedral which houses the mystery of life.

We acquire our commonality from our precious planet. We are connected to our planet at every stage of our lives. As my body changes there is an aging process where it seems my cells are hearing a call from within to one day end their continuance of Lyle. Each morning my strong S.O.S. interacts positively with my cells. I know there will be a day when my last breath is given up and at that moment my cells will respond to a mystery from within that my S.O.S. couldn't override. A new understanding of our commonality will allow us all to feel "at home" on this gorgeous and mysterious planet. Feeling "at home" here on this awesome planet requires us to acknowledge a globally meaningful and wonderful life. This life is only possible in our ever-changing yet precious eternal three seconds.

During my incarceration I heard prisoners longing to get out of prison. Upon my release I heard people longing to leave this mysterious planet and go to a distant heaven. If we all accept feeling "at home" in our three seconds, we could create a better existence for all of us. We are simply suspended in our precious three seconds before an inner calling ends our opportunity to be present and part of the symphony of life playing continuously in and around our planet, our home.